CULTURE SMART!
AUSTRALIA

Barry Penney

Graphic Arts Center Publishing®

First published in Great Britain 2003
by Kuperard, an imprint of Bravo Ltd.

Series Editor Geoffrey Chesler
Design DW Design

Simultaneously published in the U.S.A. and Canada
by Graphic Arts Center Publishing Company
P. O. Box 10306, Portland, OR 97296-0306

Second printing 2004

Library of Congress Cataloging-in-Publication Data

Penney, Barry.
Australia : a quick guide to culture and etiquette / Barry Penney.
    p. cm. — (Culture smart!)
ISBN 1-55868-774-2 (softbound)
1. Australia—Social life and customs. 2. Etiquette—Australia. 3.
National characteristics, Australian. 4. Australia—Guidebooks. I.
Title. II. Series.
DU107.P385 2003
994—dc22
                                2003019211

Printed in Hong Kong

Cover image: Sydney Harbor Bridge and Opera House.
Travel Ink/Trevor Creighton

The image on page 21 is reproduced by permission of
The Natural History Museum, London.

The photograph on page 99 is reproduced with the
permission of the Eardley family.

CultureShock!Consulting and **Culture Smart!** guides both contribute
to and regularly feature in the weekly travel program "Fast Track"
on BBC World TV.

About the Author

BARRY PENNEY is an Australian teacher, trainer, and management executive. A graduate of the University of Adelaide, he first worked in education before specializing in sales, sales management, and marketing for a number of multinational corporations. He went on to study at The Australian Administrative Staff College, Victoria. He has lived and worked in the United States, the United Kingdom, and Turkey. On returning to Australia he established a management training business. He has devised and conducted marketing and presentation courses, has published several short stories, and teaches English to foreign language students. He is an Associate Fellow of the Australian Institute of Management.

Other Books in the Series

- Culture Smart! Britain
- Culture Smart! China
- Culture Smart! Finland
- Culture Smart! France
- Culture Smart! Germany
- Culture Smart! Greece
- Culture Smart! Hong Kong
- Culture Smart! India
- Culture Smart! Ireland
- Culture Smart! Italy
- Culture Smart! Japan
- Culture Smart! Korea

- Culture Smart! Mexico
- Culture Smart! Netherlands
- Culture Smart! Philippines
- Culture Smart! Poland
- Culture Smart! Russia
- Culture Smart! Singapore
- Culture Smart! Spain
- Culture Smart! Sweden
- Culture Smart! Switzerland
- Culture Smart! Thailand
- Culture Smart! USA

Other titles are in preparation. For more information, contact: info@kuperard.co.uk

The publishers would like to thank **CultureShock!**Consulting for its help in researching and developing the concept for this series.

CultureShock!Consulting

We are all likely at some time to be dealing with other cultures—foreign visitors at home, e-mails from abroad, overseas sales agents, multicultural teams within our organization, or a new foreign management structure.

CultureShock!Consulting creates tailor-made seminars and consultancy programs to meet all types of corporate, public sector, and individual intercultural needs. It provides pre- and post-assignment programs, as well as ongoing "in-the-field" counseling worldwide.

For details, see www.cultureshockconsulting.com

contents

contents

Map of Australia

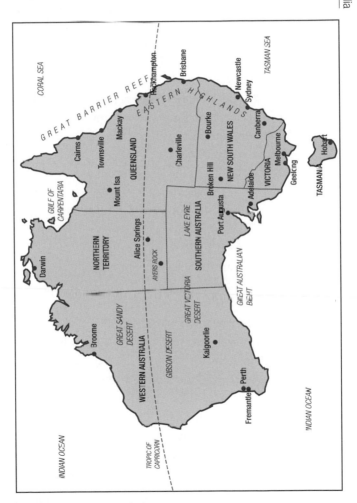

introduction

What makes Australia different? First, if you're traveling from Southeast Asia, you'll cover about 4,500 miles (7,240 km); if from the Americas or South Africa, about 9,000 miles (14,500 km); if from Europe, about 10,500 miles (17,000 km). It's not just a quick crossing by ferryboat, or a walk over a bridge. It's a long way to "Down Under." So there are bound to be cultural as well as geographical differences.

And then there's the size of it. It's a long way from one side to the other. Perth, the capital of Western Australia, is the most isolated city in the world. It is closer to Singapore than to Sydney, which is about 1,900 miles (3,000 km) away.

Most countries have probably had a fairly steady population growth, with much the same ethnic mix, for hundreds of years. Apart, of course, from the Aborigines, who have been there for over fifty thousand years, Australians have not been there long. The first Europeans settled just over two hundred years ago; most other immigrants arrived less than fifty years ago. Australia's population has doubled since 1957, transforming what was perhaps one of the dullest nations to one of the most stimulating, with many interesting differences of culture and custom.

Australians are generally warmhearted and generous. Perhaps they have taken the best from the immigrant cultures, blending them with the best of Aboriginal and early settler cultures—and, of course, also keeping a little of what was not the best. But Australians are mostly open, honest, and forthright, and will expect you to be the same. Early life in Australia was difficult; the result is an ethic of hard work and hard play. Australians work to live.

Today, Australia has one of the world's highest standards of living, fine food and wine, a great sporting tradition, a colorful and invigorating multiculturalism, and an affection for visitors.

This book sets out to provide more than just the nuts and bolts of where to stay, what to see, and how to travel. Culture Smart! guides are written for true travelers who want to understand the beliefs and attitudes of the people they meet: to learn from them, and to absorb the human dimension of the country. *Culture Smart! Australia* provides the necessary background information to enable you to put a human face on the country and its people; to communicate; to make friends; to share experiences; to enjoy the culture; and to form lasting relationships.

Key Facts

Official Name	Commonwealth of Australia	Member of the British Commonwealth
Capital City	Canberra	
Main Cities	Sydney, Melbourne, Brisbane, Adelaide, Perth, Hobart, Darwin.	
Area	2,966,136 sq. miles (7,682,300 sq. km)	
Climate	Ranges from tropical to temperate. Most of Australia is arid land or desert.	The extreme north is tropical; the southeast and southwest more Mediterranean. The east coast and the Eastern Highlands are the areas of greatest rainfall.
Population	19,727,500	
Ethnic Makeup	Nationals from over 140 countries. Predominantly European descent.	40% of population are immigrants or children of immigrants; 25% were born overseas.
Family Makeup	Average family size 2.7; Average number of children 1.74.	
Language	English	Aboriginal and other languages are spoken at home and are available in government offices, banks, insurance houses, etc.
Religion	Roman Catholics 50%; Other Christian denominations 24.3%.	Other religions incl. Eastern Orthodox, Jews, Muslims, and Hindus.

Government	Democratic Federal system comprising six states and two territories.	The states are New South Wales, Queensland, South Australia, Victoria, Western Australia, and Tasmania. The territories are the Northern Territory and the Australian Capital Territory.
Seat of Federal Government	Canberra	
Media	There are 144 radio outlets nationally and TV has 250 services nationally. Special Broadcasting Services (SBS) broadcasts in 68 languages.	Australia is said to have the highest newspaper/ magazine readership in the world.
Electricity	240 volts	Three-pronged plugs used. Adaptors are needed for most overseas appliances.
Video/TV	Pal B system	Some systems will play NTSC TV.
Telephone	Australia's country code is 61.	International and state codes are listed at the back of the telephone directory.
Currency	Australian dollar	
Time Difference	Australia has three time zones. Some areas have Daylight Saving.	Western: GMT+8 hrs Central: GMT+9.5 hrs Eastern: GMT+10 hrs For Daylight Saving add one hour.

chapter one

LAND &
PEOPLE

Australia is the world's largest island and its smallest continent. This is a country the size of the United States of America, spanning three time zones, yet with barely nineteen million inhabitants. It is an ancient land, geologically one of the oldest on earth, and was first populated by the Aborigines and Torres Strait Islanders.

These original inhabitants are thought to have come south from Asia some fifty to seventy thousand years ago, when Australia was linked to Indonesia by a land bridge. In 1788 a handful of Europeans arrived. Before 1788 Australia had been of interest to the Netherlands, Spain, and France, but after the voyages of Captain James Cook it was the British who were the colonizers. Convicts and subsequently free settlers from Britain and Ireland arrived to establish a thriving Anglo-Celtic society.

The early Europeans brought with them epidemics of smallpox, measles, and venereal diseases, and they also, occasionally, murdered Aborigines. At the time of white settlement the estimated black population was 700,000. By 1900, this figure had shrunk to 100,000. Much has been done in recent times, and much is still being done, to repair the damage.

Throughout the 1800s freed convicts, explorers, and settlers spread across the continent. Wheat growing, sheep and cattle ranching, the discovery of gold, and expanding immigration all contributed to spectacular economic growth.

From 1945, after the end of the Second World War, the immigration of many of Europe's dispossessed began what was to be one of the world's greatest exercises in multiculturalism.

Convict Ancestry

Most of those Australians who can claim convict ancestry have become quite proud of it. The fact is that, although described as "felons," these convicts had committed no serious crimes by today's definition of the word. Their offenses would be better described as "misdemeanors." In those days, stealing a sheep to feed one's family was a hanging offense. Those who were sent on the long, terrible voyage to Australia were recorded to have committed such offenses as stealing a round of cheese, a loaf of bread, or some lace handkerchiefs, or even opening a letter addressed to someone else.

This has been added to in recent years by an influx of immigrants from Asia, South Africa, the old U.S.S.R., the Mediterranean, and continental Europe. Today, just over a quarter of Australia's population was not born there.

In 1988 the nation of Australia celebrated its Bicentennial—the two hundredth anniversary of the arrival of the first convict ships. As with the United States and Canada, also first colonized by the British, the Europeans displaced a native population that had been there for thousands of years. And, like the United States and Canada, Australia has become a powerful, industrialized nation with a high standard of living.

Settled and populated by Europeans for the first one hundred and fifty years, Australia was traditionally tied to Europe—and in particular to the mother country, Great Britain. In the last thirty years or so, nearby Asian nations have become increasingly important. Australia has begun a shift in foreign policy and trade focus from Europe to Asia, including general tariff reductions and the promotion of an Asia-Pacific free trade area by the year 2020.

This, then, is the young country we shall examine—in its transition from wild frontier land to modern industrialized nation, and in the transformation this has wrought on its people.

TERRAIN

Australia is the only nation to occupy an entire continent—albeit the smallest of the seven continents. Surrounded by the Indian Ocean and the South Pacific, it is also an island—of 2,966,136 square miles (7,682,300 sq. km).

The island/continent lies southeast of the Asian landmass, bordered on the north by the Timor Sea, beyond which lie the islands of Papua New Guinea and Indonesia—the closest neighbors. To

the east, the Coral Sea separates Australia from
the island chain called the Solomon Islands, and
the Tasman Sea separates it from
New Zealand. On the west lies the
Indian Ocean.

The sixth largest country on
Earth, Australia extends
approximately 2,500 miles
(approximately 4,000 km) from
east to west, and 1,875 miles
(3,000 km) from north to south.
The highest point is Mount
Kosciusko, at 7,310 feet (2,228 m); the lowest
point is Lake Eyre, at 39 feet (12 m) below
sea level.

From east to west, Australia has four main
geographical regions. The eastern lowland plain
stretches from Cape York Peninsula in the north
to the city of Melbourne in the south. Much of
this area is forested. A few miles off the northern
shore is the Great Barrier Reef, the largest coral
reef in the world, which runs 1,200 miles (1,900
km) along the coast. On the southern part of the
plain are the cities of Brisbane, Sydney, Canberra,
and Melbourne—and Hobart in Tasmania.

The Eastern Highlands is a ridge of hills and
mountains that separate the lowlands from the
interior. It includes the tropical mountain
hinterland of Queensland, the hills of New

England, the Blue Mountains, the Australian Alps in New South Wales and Victoria, and the mountains that dominate most of Tasmania.

West of the highlands lie the central plains. This is a region of dry depressions, or basins, the largest of which, the Great Artesian Basin, extends from the Gulf of Carpentaria in the north to the mouth of the Murray River in the south—the largest inland drainage system in the world.

The Western Plateau covers the western part of the continent with rocky ridges and plains, and large, forbidding deserts (the Great Sandy, the Gibson, the Great Victoria, and the Tanami). In the north, jungle and swamps cover Arnhem Land on the shore of the Gulf of Carpentaria. In the south, the Nullarbor (meaning "no trees") Plain borders the Great Australian Bight.

CLIMATE

Remember that Australia lies in the Southern Hemisphere, with seasons that are opposite those in the north—July is the middle of winter and January the peak of summer. Most of Australia is warm and dry, the southern part being the most comfortable, with temperatures in Melbourne averaging 48°F (9°C) in its July winter to 68°F (20°C) in January. Adelaide is similar, Perth a little warmer. Temperatures in Darwin average 77°F

(25°C) in July and 86°F (30°C) in January. The interior of Australia often reaches 100°F (38°C) and can go as high as 115°F (46°C).

The largest city, Sydney, has a subtropical climate, warm to hot and wet in summer, up to 95°F (35°C) and mild, dry winters, up to 77°F (25°C). Canberra's temperatures average 68°F (20°C) in January and 42°F (6°C) in July.

Northern Australia (beyond the Tropic of Capricorn) is subject to an extreme tropical wet/dry weather pattern. What this means is that from November to April there are torrential downpours, monsoonal storms, and high humidity in the city of Darwin and the northern cities and towns of Queensland.

Rainfall is lowest in the center (about 40 percent of the continent is desert), with less than 10 inches (25 cm) per year. Sheep and cattle stations (ranches) are found on the edges of these deserts. Crops mostly grow where the rainfall exceeds 10 inches (25 cm). Rainfall is greatest in the northeast tropical rainforest areas, with upwards of 59 inches (150 cm). In the south, Tasmania and Victoria receive more than 30 inches (76 cm), Adelaide and Perth less.

There is little that is ordinary about Australia. The extremes in climate from torrential rain to disastrous drought, and the ever-present threat of bushfires, along with the isolation of the continent for fifty million years, have combined to promote the country's rich and diverse native fauna and flora. Kangaroos of various sizes and colors, wallabies, and other oddities, such as the kookaburra, koala, platypus, echidna, galah, and many of the brightly colored parrots, are be found naturally nowhere else in the world. The ubiquitous Australian gum tree, or eucalyptus, which is dependent on bushfires for its survival and propagation, has been exported for use over much of the world, generally because of its thirst: its deep tap roots help to drain swamps and marshland.

AUSTRALIA'S ABORIGINES

It should be noted that Australia's Aboriginal peoples were not a single group of people. They were made up of at least six hundred widely scattered language groups. Some groups shared some beliefs, customs, and technological and cultural practices—the result of trade, intermarriage, and complex family connections— but there were also great differences between the groups. Even today, the Aboriginal population refers to itself as made up of many "peoples," or "nations," and it is common to talk about the

Aboriginal Peoples of Australia when referring to them historically.

The Dreamtime

The Australian Aboriginal creation myths tell of "The Dreamtime," a time before history, when legendary, totemic Ancestral Beings sang the world into existence, and in doing so created the world and everything in it— plants, animals, landscape features, humans, and the customs and laws of those humans. Stories of the Dreamtime vary greatly from tribe to tribe, and from region to region, but the notion of the totemic ancestor is remarkably persistent. Images of these are to be found on the walls of rock shelters and caves in many parts of the country—the Aborigines are responsible for what is probably the world's greatest collection of rock art—and many different groups still use stories of the Dreamtime to explain the shape of a landform, the characteristic of a particular animal, or the existence of a particular law.

The Impact of the Settlers

At first the Aborigines showed little interest in assimilating into European society. Instead they expected the Europeans to continue their "Walkabout" and move on, or adopt the superior Aboriginal ways. But the tide rolled on, as it had done in the United States, in Canada, and wherever Europeans displaced indigenous people.

Aborigines and Europeans related to the land in completely opposing ways. The Aborigines were generally hunters and gatherers, although some groups were engaged in agricultural practices; the Europeans were farmers, who regarded the land as theirs for the taking because it was not being cultivated. The Aborigines were simply ignored by the Europeans, who declared Australia an empty and ownerless land, "*terra nullius.*" They were, as John Pilger put it in *A Secret Country*, considered not as human but rather as "part of the fauna." It was only in 1992 that the Australian High Court ruled that the Aborigines' title to the land had not been extinguished. Today, Australian Aborigines drive cars, or ride in trains, over the land they once trod so carefully.

The Aborigines realized, as the settlers kept coming, that the newcomers wanted to own the land, not to share it, and that they were here to stay—along with their fences, their missionaries to convert them, their politicians to interfere with them, their Community Service bureaucrats to take their children into care, their governments to palm them off with rather useless tracts of land, and their alcohol. Many Aborigines exchanged work for food and lodgings, particularly on farms and in rural areas. Later came unemployment payouts and other cash benefits, meaning that many Aborigines had no real need to work, and there was ready access to alcohol. Successive governments, through a lack of understanding of how to cope with the problems of Aboriginals, contributed disaster along with benefit.

They had no immunity to the diseases the settlers introduced, and their numbers suffered accordingly. There were also murders. The most famous, perhaps, was the Myall Creek Massacre in 1838, when Aborigines—men, women, and children—were rounded up after some perceived wrongdoing (perhaps, as was often the case, they had taken a sheep to feed themselves), herded into a creek bed, and shot. We don't know how many there were, but there may have been hundreds. For this wanton killing of defenseless Aborigines, seven of the eleven whites accused were subsequently hanged. But such justice was not common.

From around the early 1900s a sort of cruel benevolence grew out of missionary interference and government ignorance, resulting in the white authorities' removal of Aboriginal children, particularly those of mixed blood (usually the result of white men's abuse of black women), from their families. This was an attempt to integrate them "for their own good" into white society. Descendants from this "Stolen Generation," as it is called, are still searching for their roots, trying to discover who they really are.

There is now a great deal of concern for Aboriginal welfare. For most Australians, and for the visitor, this is a topic of great sensitivity and uncertainty. There is regret for what has been done, and for official ineptitude in the face of infant mortality rates, alcoholism, and family violence. While it is quite possible to live in Australia without getting to know any Aborigines—and, for those who live in the major cities, without actually seeing any—the problems of the Aborigines are always there. Most Australians abhor, and are embarrassed by, the fact of a disadvantaged underclass, marginalized and living on the fringes of society despite the spending of huge sums of money by recent governments. But there is also, among the ignorant and ill informed—mostly, but not entirely, outside the cities, and particularly in the north and northwest—a small, residual, hard core of racism that the Australians themselves call "redneck" ignorance.

The Aborigines Today

Many Aboriginal communities are dynamic and self-determining. This is particularly the case where they have made successful claims to their traditional land, and now live on that land. Some communities support internationally recognized art centers where artists produce works that sell around the world, often for thousands of dollars. Other communities manage farmland, parkland, and mining leases.

Aborigines have been very successful activists, particularly over the last forty years. In 1967 they won the right to vote in what was the most unequivocal referendum held in Australia; in 1971 Aboriginal Neville Bonner was elected to the Senate; in 1972 Tent Embassy was set up outside Parliament to advance the cause of land rights (the returning of traditional lands); in 1992 a High Court decision, known as Mabo, rejected the notion of *terra nullius* and affirmed that Aboriginal people were in possession of the land prior to 1788; in the late 1990s the notion of Reconciliation (coming to terms with wrongs of the past as related to the treatment of Aborigines) was embraced by many Australians.

There are many highly successful Aboriginal people in Australian public life. They include Cathy Freeman (an Olympic medallist), Mick and Pat Dodson (activists), Deborah Mailman (an actor), Aden Ridgeway (a politician), Lowitja O'Donohue (an activist and bureaucrat, who has been put forward on a number of occasions as contender for position of Governor-General), Ernie Dingo (an actor and television personality), Archie Roach (a singer), and Pat O'Shane (a magistrate).

Nevertheless, you would be well advised to approach the subject of the Aboriginal Peoples with great caution. Read about it, and try to understand. Ask questions, by all means, and listen.

THE AUSTRALIANS

The arrival of the First Fleet of eleven ships from Britain in 1788, carrying over thirteen hundred people, began the influx of different cultures to Australia. First came English seamen and soldiers, along with English and Irish convicts. These were followed by free settlers, mostly from England—

ethnically and culturally Celtic and Anglo-Saxon—and a significant number of Chinese, who arrived to try their luck on the goldfields during the great gold rush of the 1850s. Between 1851 and 1860 the rate of immigration was fifty thousand per annum. The immigrants and the Aborigines mostly went their separate ways.

Postwar immigration brought a wide variety of Europeans from war-torn Europe—six million since 1945. Australia implemented a policy of free passage for United Kingdom residents, and assisted passage for ex-servicemen from the British Isles, the U.S.A., the Netherlands, Norway, France, Belgium, and Denmark. From 1950 to 1960 economic and humanitarian events also opened the gates to Germany, Turkey, Yugoslavia, Chile (after Allende), and Indochina (after the Vietnam war).

Since the 1960s the population of Australia has grown, mainly from immigration from over 120 countries, including, in order: the British Isles, New Zealand, Italy, Croatia, Serbia, Slovenia, Bosnia/Macedonia, Greece, Germany, Vietnam, Poland, and Lebanon.

This mixture of ethnic and cultural origins has resulted in the most multicultural mixture of people in the world. They call themselves Australians.

GOVERNMENT AND POLITICS
Australia is divided into six states (New South Wales, Queensland, South Australia, Victoria, Western Australia, and Tasmania) and two territories (the Northern Territory and the Australian Capital Territory—in which is located the Federal Capital, Canberra).

Until late in the nineteenth century, these areas were separately governed British colonies. In the late 1800s, Australians realized the advantages to be gained by becoming one unified nation. A constitution was drawn up and approved by the British Parliament in 1901, reflecting the country's British origin and based on the Westminster system of government.

The King or Queen of England is the official head of state, and has formal power but little direct authority over Australian laws and government. The Governor-General is the monarch's representative.

As in the U.K. and Canada, the Prime Minister is the leader of the party that has the most members elected to the parliament, which is divided into upper and lower houses. The lower house, the House of Representatives, has 148 members elected for a three-year term and is essentially the legislative body. Only this house can propose and pass bills that affect government money and spending. The upper house, the Senate, has seventy-six members—twelve from each state and two from each territory. Those from states serve six-year terms; those from territories serve three-year terms.

There are several political parties in Australia, each embracing a political philosophy different from the others. This difference is actually more noticeable between minor parties such as the Greens and the Democrats, and between them and the two main parties, than between the two main parties. These are the Labor Party (with a history arising from its roots in trade unions and blue-collar workers), and the Liberal/National Country Party coalition (with a history arising from roots in the farming community and industrialists and white-collar workers). Voting for these two tends to be within the range of 47 to 53 percent. They have become close in ideology.

Politics is the subject of much discussion in Australia, at least in part because voting is compulsory. And it is interesting to note that it is not the voting that is compulsory, but visiting the polling booth to have your name crossed off. What this means, of course, is that a person can simply attend, and then either fail to fill out a voting form or provide a "donkey vote" (mark the paper in a humorous or even obscene way). The important thing is that the number of donkey votes is insignificant. Australians take their voting seriously, and in the main know exactly what they are voting for.

"Talk-back" radio is bigger in Australia, perhaps, than anywhere else in the world, and many people listen avidly; particularly country folk, workers who can have the radio on in factories, garages, workshops, and the like; and stay-at-home moms. Listeners are kept very much up to date on current affairs and politics.

Regarding political debate, as a visitor you would be well advised to question and listen, but you should, of course, be careful when expressing opinions on local politics. Where you can make a contribution is in a discussion of the politics of your own country. You might be surprised by how much Australians know about world affairs. The news in Australia, in the newspapers, on the radio, and on television, and particularly through SBS— Special Broadcasting Services—contains much more overseas news than is generally found in other countries. The Australians like to keep up with what is going on.

Historical Snapshot

1770
Captain Cook lands at Botany Bay, and calls the eastern coastline New South Wales.

1788
Captain Arthur Phillip and the First Fleet arrive, with convicts.

1793
The first free settlers arrive.

1803
Matthew Flinders circumnavigates the mainland.

1840
Abolition of convict transportation to New South Wales.

1851
Gold discovered in Victoria and New South Wales.

1897–8
New and separate Australian Constitution prepared.

1899
Constitution approved by ballot of the people.

1900
Federation of Australian Colonies—British approval.
Melbourne becomes temporary capital of the new nation.

1901
January 1: Australia declared an independent Commonwealth within the British Empire. Local voting for local parliament.

1908
Canberra (midway between Melbourne and Sydney) chosen as the permanent Federal Capital.

1914
Australia enters World War I.

1915
More than 8,000 Australian soldiers lost in battle of Gallipoli in Turkey; 62,000 Australian lives lost in World War I.

1920
QANTAS (Queensland and Northern Territory Aerial Services) founded.

1928
Royal Flying Doctor Service established.

1939
Australia enters World War II.

1942
Darwin bombed by the Japanese on February 19, 1943.

1947
Australian government buys all shares in QANTAS.

1956
Olympic Games held in Melbourne.

1965
Australian soldiers sent to the Vietnam conflict.

1967
Referendum sees 90 percent of Australians say "yes" to the right of Aborigines to vote.

1973
Opening of the Sydney Opera House.

1975
Governor-General John Kerr sacks Prime Minister Gough Whitlam.

1983
Australia II wins the America's Cup yacht race.

1993
Native Title Act passed to help Aborigines press land claims.

2000
Olympic Games held in Sydney.

chapter two

VALUES &
ATTITUDES

"FAIR DINKUM"

Australia is an ethnic melting pot—but it wasn't
always that way. Beliefs like being "fair dinkum"
(being honest, up-front, a person who keeps to his
or her word) go back to the pioneering days. That
is not to say that the phrase is inappropriate
today, because immigrants were quick to pick it
up. The fact is that those immigrant converts to
what epitomized the Australian way of life (or
what Australians like to think is peculiar to their
way of life) seemed to take it up with a new
intensity. No more "fair dinkum Aussies" exist
than those who left the postwar awfulness of
Europe for sunnier shores.

Equally, it wasn't long before the Australians
noticed that these new arrivals worked a bit
harder than they were accustomed to themselves,
and that they prospered. For example, they
observed that those from the Mediterranean built
themselves very big brick houses with lots of tiles
and marble, and balustrades on verandas and
staircases. At first this gave rise to some envy-

based criticism from a more laid-back Australian working community. This was fairly quickly replaced by a desire that they, too, should have a big house with all these trimmings.

It is, perhaps, fair to say that early immigrants brought with them, and inculcated into Australia, a new, or at least a stronger, work ethic.

WORKING TO LIVE VERSUS LIVING TO WORK

During the 1990s, an Australian who worked for an American company was visited by a senior executive from the U.S.A. The visitor asked him to arrange for the management team to join him for a breakfast meeting on Sunday morning. "Bloody hell!" the Australian thought (see Chapter 9, Communicating), knowing that there was no way his team would give up their golf tee-off time, their early swim with the kids, the start of the yacht race, or simply breakfast in bed with the wife—just for a *meeting!*

The Australian, a quick thinker, said: "It probably wouldn't be a good idea. I don't think they would be too impressed about missing church. And to some of them, even the *idea* of working on the Sabbath. . ."

The meeting was scheduled for Monday morning!

It is not that Australians do not work long hours (a myth perpetuated by many writers), but that Americans work even longer hours. According to recent OECD (Organization for Economic Cooperation and Development) figures, Australians are in the top three industrialized nations in numbers of hours worked: 1870 per year, just behind Japan (1889), and America (1958).

There is not a problem with the number of hours worked, but the majority of Australians do not happily give up their "living" time. That's why they work: to live—to enjoy the weather, the beaches, the sports, and the socializing.

Should you gain employment in Australia, you will be expected (by other workers) to work the same hours as they do.

"MATESHIP"

You will notice a form of address that is used by many Australian men toward all males: "mate." "G'day, mate;" "What can I get you, mate?" This is simply a casual, cheerful greeting, with no great overtones of friendship.

True "mateship" was traditionally something quite different; in fact it was almost mystical. It grew out of a feeling of fellowship between men who were facing or had lived through extreme or difficult conditions or great adversity together. It was the brotherhood that came from the sharing of any significant experience, such as fighting together in wartime. As one old soldier said, "The blokes in the trenches were not all friends, but they were all mates. We knew we would all go over the top of the trenches together." At a later stage, perhaps, mateship could come from a different kind of hardship, such getting drunk together, and one man having the courage to take his mate home to face an irate wife. Aussies think, "Only a real mate would do that." Women were excluded from mateship: a man would never think of addressing a woman as "mate," and he would never consider her to be one. Women themselves would never use the term.

Australians inherited from their British forebears a capacity for self-mockery. However, many fell for the Pioneer image that is associated with the mateship ethos, and still like to see themselves in the *Crocodile Dundee* image (referring to actor Paul Hogan's hit movies of 1985 and 1988); they wear bush hats; some even wear "digger" (Australian for "soldier")-style army hats with the brim turned up on one side; they drive grimy, four-wheel-drive vehicles; and swear they have lived on witchetty grubs and goanna (lizard) steaks.

Nowadays this kind of exclusiveness has made mateship seem rather old-fashioned. It is also worth noting that the term "mate" is sometimes used ironically, to indicate relationships—such as may occur in criminal or political circles—that are not necessarily upfront and honest.

The reality of mateship today is that it comes to the fore in times of crisis, and is manifested as a general sense of cooperation and a "fix-it" attitude among all Australians, men and women. In the bushfires that affected much of Canberra and northern Victoria in 2003, over two thousand volunteer firefighters (many of them women) simply left their jobs, donned their outfits, and stood side by side for days at a time, trying to protect the property of others. Australians are proud (sometimes to a fault, especially when traveling overseas) and independent, but they come together in a crisis, lending a hand to help their mates.

"CULTURAL CRINGE" AND "TALL POPPIES"

You might have heard of these two Aussie characteristics. You should ignore them, or be prepared to seem very dated. There was a time when Australians thought that anything American, British, or European must be better than its Australian counterpart. Probably this was the case, many years ago. This self-deprecation gave birth to a kind of social embarrassment, or so-called "cultural cringe."

At about the time of the Melbourne Olympics, in 1956, when visitors exclaimed how well the games worked, how well Australia did, how interesting the museums and art galleries were, and how much they enjoyed the theater, Australians began to see themselves as having caught up, culturally. Unfortunately, this perceived success in the arts, as well as in moviemaking, in pop music, and, above all, in sport, resulted in overconfidence, evident in some Australians, particularly when overseas. Maybe a bit of "cringe" was not such a bad thing.

In days long gone by, many Australians liked to think of themselves as Little Aussie Battlers—working-class people struggling against upper-class bosses. However, when one of those battlers "made it" by achieving success, fame, or money, he became "one of them Tall Poppies"—and Tall Poppies needed to be cut down to size. Today, however, it is fine, even admirable, to achieve success, provided that you do not forget your mates or your beginnings.

RELIGION

In a recent census, in response to the optional question on religion, approximately 68 percent of the population were found to be Christian, of whom 46 percent were Catholic or Anglican (Church of England); the rest were made up of different Protestant denominations. Some 1.5 percent were Muslim, and 2 percent Buddhist. What is perhaps most interesting is that 25 percent stated that they had no religion, or gave no answer.

Generally, church attendance in Australia is falling quite dramatically. Religion is one of those sacred cows that are more the butt of humor than the subject of serious discussions. While attitudes to right and wrong at a social, moral level have their foundation in Judeo-Christian values—for example, a reluctance to steal, lie, or cheat (or at least to be caught doing so)—these are not generally seen as religious mores. Giving someone "a fair go," and "looking after your mate" would probably be more readily given reasons for doing the right thing.

Overall, religion is not taken very seriously by the masses, and rarely would workmates at any level need to know, or even care, what religion the others are.

However, as with anywhere in the world, you would need to know your company very well before entering into critical debate on the subject.

HUMOR

It is an article of faith in Australia that all visitors must be able to take a joke. Learn to laugh at yourself, your country, and so on—and if you really want to be a social hit, tell jokes against yourself, your country, and the way you speak.

Nothing is sacred. There is almost nothing that cannot be laughed at. Particularly good things to poke fun at are religion and religious hierarchy, politics and politicians, Australians (provided you are Australian—Australian humor is often very self-deprecating), Poms (British people—even weak jokes will do), and all sacred cows. The important things of life are taken very lightly. Sport, however, is taken very seriously!

The Australian humorist best-known internationally is probably Barry Humphries, who has the distinction of convincing most Americans that she is Dame Edna Everidge—for real.

Recently, the "Good Weekend" supplement to the *Sydney Morning Herald* asked a number of experts—well-known Australians from the arts, the legal fraternity, some members of parliament, and the like—what it means to say, "That's unAustralian." What came up? Certainly not the humor. Here are some of the answers:

It's unAustralian:

- to know all the words to "Advance Australia Fair" (the national anthem).

- to leave the pub when the lights are still on.

- to judge Australian movies by the same criteria as Hollywood movies.

- to stop for pedestrians when turning left on to a crossing.

- to think cricket might be a better game if a match lasted, say, ninety minutes, instead of about a year.

- to live in England for two years and ever to go out of London.

- to feel foreign criticism of Australia is fair.

- to pronounce foreigners' names correctly.

- to actually know someone from another culture, other than Mai Ling from the mailroom.

- not to add an "o" to your mate's first name (unless he's called Antonio, in which case you call him "Ant").

ATTITUDES TO OTHERS

Most Australians are saddened by the plight of those Aboriginal people who have remained disadvantaged in various ways as a result of the coming of the European settlers. Not only do they not know what to do about those who have been lost to culture change—lost to alcohol, family violence, disease, and high infant mortality rates—but they also feel guilty. A few racist bigots ignore the successful among them and blame the Aborigines for being lazy, ignorant, uncivilized, and unintelligent.

It is, of course, difficult, if not impossible, to lump together the attitudes of all Australians. "All Australians" includes those of Continental European immigrant stock; those who are of English stock and are actually proud of it; those republicans who are of English stock and want to forget it; those of Aboriginal stock who just want to be recognized; and those of Asian stock, who must be vastly bewildered by all of the above. But the following may help you, the visitor, just a little bit, to understand some general attitudes.

Most Australians have nothing against the British (although you will sometimes hear the words "Brit" or "Brits" used disparagingly). That is, they have nothing against the Welsh, the Scottish, or the Irish. They may, however, have something against the English.

In the early postwar years there was a great deal of immigration from England. Many English folk were placed in some pretty awful new towns (Elizabeth in South Australia was one), far from the sea and the beaches they saw as typifying Australia. They gained a reputation for "whingeing" (grumbling) that things were not the same as they were back home. Many Australians offered to pay for their return. These English immigrants were given the name "Poms" (origin obscure), and, in particular, "whingeing Poms."

Yes, it *was* a bit like that. Today, most of the younger Australians have forgotten why the Poms simply have to be the butt of all jokes. It's a bit rough on the new immigrants—the older ones have learned to give it back. The term "Poms" is nowadays mostly reserved for use in the Test (cricket) Matches between the two countries, and is almost affectionate. Despite the rise in republican sentiment, some 50 percent of the Australian public are monarchists, and are happy to have the Queen of England as Head of State.

Australians have generally liked Continental Europeans because *they* don't much like the English. And because of their antipasto, mozzarella, risotto, hummus, soccer, Greek salad, dancing with handkerchiefs . . .

Australians like Asians because they are gentle; their children are amazingly well behaved; they

are thin, and set dieting challenges; and because of
Yum Cha, Peking duck, lemongrass, sambals,
satay, sushi . . .

Australians like Americans because they are
much like Australians. Their
background as pioneers is similar,
and it shows in their self-confidence,
loud laughter, willing handshake,
and general friendliness. And
most Australians believe the Yanks
saved them from Japanese invasion in
World War II.

Despite Australia's tolerance,
however, the issue of refugees is an extremely
sensitive one. A great many people believe that
asylum seekers should not be admitted at all, or
should be put in detention centers. Visitors
should tread very carefully here.

Since the terrorist attack on September 11,
2001, by Islamic fundamentalists, some followers
of Islam in Australia have suffered verbal abuse
and ridicule from the lunatic fringe. Until then,
Asian Muslims who wore Islamic dress were
accepted with no more than the glance that may
be given to anyone whose appearance is strikingly
different, but terrorism has changed that.

A great deal of effort is being made by the
government and religious and other bodies to
allay fears, which are to be found at the root of

any prejudice. Most Australians abhor what they refer to as "redneck" racism.

Attitudes to Women

Australian women are out of the kitchen. As elsewhere, the opportunities offered to women have increased, and women are now active in politics, law, medical practice, universities, and, perhaps most important, business, where they are directly and immediately in competition with men. The original "Sheila" has disappeared—or is now unrecognizable in a trim charcoal business suit.

Attitudes to Each Other

Australians' attitudes to each other have changed little. There is still a strong sense of egalitarianism, and it is true that you can be talking to someone in a pub, or at a dinner party, or a barbecue, and be quite unaware that they are very important or very rich. D. H. Lawrence observed of Australia, that " . . . whereas some people felt 'better off' than others, nobody felt better than anyone else." And a British officer is known to have remarked of Australian soldiers that they "only saluted the officers that they liked."

There is a general dislike of those who exercise authority where this is felt to be undeserved or inappropriate, and this attitude is also seen in a frequent breaking of petty, unpopular, or seemingly pointless rules.

And you, the visitor, or new arrival? You will find that, if you keep your sense of humor and show a lively interest in the land and the people, Australians will take to you. As a visitor to their homes you will be warmly welcomed—as long as you keep quiet about being very wealthy, very educated, or very important.

chapter three

THE AUSTRALIANS AT HOME

HOME OWNERSHIP

"A home of my own" has for years been the great Australian dream. For around 70 percent of Australians the dream has come true, and they own their own home, or the mortgage servicing it. But it is becoming more difficult. House prices have risen disproportionately in relation to incomes over recent years. Housing developments around the cities have engulfed much of the available land, and new-home buyers have been driven further away from the city centers, creating huge suburban sprawls around Sydney and Melbourne. There is a shortage of land closer to the cities and their amenities, and this has contributed to the great increase in the building of high-rise apartment complexes (apartments are called "flats units" in Australia). These generally cluster near the city, along train lines and bus routes, and near the beaches.

The Federal government has decided to help its people meet their expectations, offering a grant to first-home buyers of $7,000, to help younger buyers purchase their first home and to stimulate home building and ancillary trades.

RENTING

Here is the story in brief. The concept of owning one's own home has recently changed. Some years ago, when interest rates on borrowed money were high and the stock market was booming with gains, investment advisors advocated renting a home and investing one's available capital elsewhere. Many Australians followed that advice. Now the stock market is seriously down, and returns on investments are low. At the same time, interest rates on loans are low, and as a consequence of these two factors people are going back to buying their own homes. This is borne out by the fact that an anticipated drop in house building applications (in line with the generally poor state of the economy) has not occurred. Thus Australians are back to their dream—owning their own home.

HOUSE STYLES

When the settlers built towns and cities in the late eighteenth and early nineteenth centuries, they built homes that resembled the ones they had left behind. Fine examples of Victorian architecture can be found in older and mostly inner-city suburban areas, such as Paddington in Sydney, Fitzroy in Melbourne, and in many country towns. Still admired by some, they sell at high prices. However, thin and squeezed together as they were, they must have looked out of place in Australia's open landscapes, and they failed to take advantage of the climate, with its abundant sunshine and balmy breezes.

If you want to see what the great Australian houses of the nineteenth century looked like, any travel agent or hotel front desk will give you information. If you are in Sydney, see Vaucluse House, after which you might enjoy drinking coffee in nearby Double Bay (known by locals as *Double Pay*), and watching fashionable Sydneysiders go by. If you are in Melbourne, visit Como House in the fashionable suburb of South Yarra.

A train ride from the city of Sydney to Parramatta, heading west, will enable you to see older suburban housing styles. In Hornsby, on the north shoreline, you will see more modern housing. In Melbourne, taking the Epping line to Clifton Hill, and changing to return to Jolimont, will provide opportunities to see similar varieties of housing. At Jolimont you can visit the famous Melbourne Cricket Ground and take a short walk back to the city via Fitzroy Gardens (where you can see Captain Cook's Cottage) and the beautiful Royal Botanical Gardens.

Later architects designed low, sprawling, ranch-type houses that were better suited to the hot, dry weather. These were single-story detached houses— known elsewhere as bungalows—set on large blocks of land. This basic six-room home is still the benchmark. Designs changed: very much in vogue are historic (and imitation) "Federation" homes, charming colonial buildings with porches and verandas all the way around, supported by pillars and with elaborately lacy wrought-iron work.

Other popular housing styles include Spanish and Mediterranean designs; wooden cottages; the Queenslander—a large, timbered, tropical house set high above ground level to allow air to circulate and with car parking underneath; and back-to-nature timber and stone structures.

Until quite recently, standard houses were traditionally built on quarter-acre (approximately one-tenth of a hectare) blocks, and in more expensive areas the blocks were bigger. As land has become scarcer, local councils have allowed smaller housing blocks—newer blocks are about half the size of the old standard.

Most living in modern Australian homes revolves around a kitchen-dining room, family room, rumpus or games room, patio, or veranda. At weekends there is a move to the backyard, by the swimming pool or barbecue. The kitchen is often of open-plan design, allowing for a great deal of social life. As a visitor you will often find yourself there, chatting with whoever is doing the cooking, and having a drink and a "nibble" (snacks with predinner drinks).

Some older houses have formal rooms for formal occasions. You may find yourself sitting in a rarely used "lounge room" and, if invited for dinner, moving to a separate dining room.

Most modern homes will have more than one "loo" (WC, toilet, lavatory) and hand basin. It is usual, if you are there for dinner, to be offered these facilities in terms of "using the bathroom" or "washing your hands." If this offer is not forthcoming, it is perfectly acceptable to ask, "May I use the bathroom?"

SUBURBAN LIVING

The southern capitals have cool to cold winters, barely above freezing point at times. Sydney and even Brisbane have cool winters. Towns in the center of Australia, like Alice Springs, can get quite cold. So despite the fact that you are going to sunny Australia you will need warm "woollies," and maybe a raincoat. Houses are mostly heated in some way in winter—not so often these days by crackling log fires, more often by portable electric or oil heaters, and occasionally by air-conditioning. Cooling comes with reverse-cycle air conditioning. Oddly enough, in the Eastern States there is less cooling than heating; although some houses do have evaporative air-cooling systems, some simply rely on fans. Most offices, restaurants, and shopping centers are air-conditioned.

Local councils provide libraries and council offices where residents can find information on building requirements and so on, and pay council taxes. These cover the cost of garbage removal (by big wheeled bins, mechanically emptied into trucks once a week, usually keeping separate paper, plastic, and kitchen waste).

Suburban living is, generally, in no way personally dangerous. A few suburbs are exceptions, and are to be avoided, and a visitor will be made aware of these exceptions. Very few of the assaults that occur are random—they are generally personal or gang related. Throughout most of the sprawling suburbs it is safe to walk the streets, and many health-conscious folk take nightly jogs, though it may be more sensible, as in most places, to do so with a friend.

There is one big exception to this matter of safety. You personally are generally safe; but your household effects are less safe. Most robberies are committed in daylight, while the owners are out or away, so when Australians leave their houses nowadays they lock all the doors and windows. (Less than thirty years ago, people rarely locked their house doors when going out—and they left their keys in their cars.)

GARDENING

Gardening is an Australian obsession. The size of the housing block means that there will be a front yard, a backyard, and a driveway down one side. The front yard is a canvas on which most Australians feel the need to paint—verdant lawns splashed with the brilliance of native flora, such as grevilleas, banksias, kangaroo's paw, and bottle brush, and imported roses, chrysanthemums, and dahlias. Most Australian couples, particularly those with young children and limited budgets, spend many hours of the weekend digging, planting, pruning, weeding, and, most of all, watering. The front yard represents the individual image that the householder wants to present to the world. Australians care what neighbors, passers-by, and visitors think of them.

When visiting Australians at home, it is important to be aware of the pride they feel in their efforts to make their place beautiful, in most cases particularly their garden. Commenting on it, and showing interest, will win you many hearts and will ensure you are welcome.

The backyard is another domain. Many Australians have a work shed in the backyard, crammed full of garden and handyman's tools: wheelbarrow, hoses, rakes, shovels, forks, paints, brushes, saws, chisels, hammers, and nails. A visitor might just be invited to see the shed, particularly if it houses an old refrigerator and some cold beer, as they often do.

The Victa Mower

In 1952, in Sydney, Mervyn Victor Richardson welded a peach tin to a miniature motor, filled it with gasoline, and attached it to a lawn mower with rotary blades. By the mid 1990s, six million Australians were mowing with a Victa.

The tools are signs of the do-it-yourself disease (DIY), which most suburban householders catch. Australian men and women are, on the whole, very handy and practical. DIY is a large industry in Australia and, to many people, heaven is the local DIY hardware emporium—vast areas stacked with every conceivable fixing thing, or replacement thing, from washers, taps, and baths, to garden sheds and "bar-b-ques."

One such "barbie" will be in the backyard—usually a gas-fired one, although a few stalwarts still have a brick-and-hotplate structure that burns wood. These traditionalists will probably show you how a handful of gum (eucalyptus) leaves thrown on the fire adds to the flavor of the meat. Try this if you use one of the many barbecues available to the public in suburban parks (run by the local councils—wood supplied), or if you are in the bush (in the country, or in scrubland on the side of the road), or at a beach. Many Australians take a portable barbecue on a country drive instead of a traditional picnic lunch. You need to be sure in summer that high temperatures have not brought about a ban on open fires. Breaking the ban carries large fines. (There is more on being invited to a barbecue in Chapter 6, Time Out.)

SCHOOLS AND SCHOOLING

Australia offers a free public education system to its over three million children. The system has three levels: elementary (from six to twelve years of age), secondary (from age twelve to fifteen or sixteen), and tertiary (university level). The names given to the levels, and the ages, vary a little from state to state. Many parents send their children to preschools or kindergartens from the age of three or four. There are a number of expensive private schools, many of them religious institutions, most of which do not limit students to followers of their religion. These provide for more than a million students. Children are required by law to attend school until they are fifteen (sixteen in Tasmania).

Australia has an educated population, in that almost every Australian over the age of ten can read and write. However, there is concern that many Australian seventeen-year-olds do not continue with their education, whereas Japanese seventeen-year-olds nearly all go on to university. Asian influence is considerable, because of the large numbers of Asian students being sent to study at Australian universities—and the large number of Asian families immigrating—who have much stronger study and work habits than Australians. Asians take far more than their proportion of top places in university entrance exams. This is, however, having the effect of providing a challenge to Australian students and raising their standards of study. Interestingly enough, many Asian parents are concerned at the ways their children also change as a result of their new environment, and take up sport to the detriment of their studies.

THE SCHOOL YEAR

The dates of school terms vary between states. As a rough guide, they tend to run as follows:

First term: end of January to the first week of April.
Second term: end of April to the end of June.
Third term: end of July to the end of September.
Fourth term: first week of October to the second week of December.

Children who live in the outback (in the country, and far away from towns), on sheep or cattle stations many miles inland, are often too far away from any school to attend classes. To cater to them, the Australian government created Schools of the Air. These schools send lessons and homework through the mail and use two-way radio to enable students and teachers to communicate during regular school hours.

You can visit a School of the Air at Broken Hill, an interesting old mining town in the far west of New South Wales. A travel agent will provide the details.

SHOPS AND SERVICES

As a broad generalization, shops open at 8:30 or 9:00 a.m. and close about 5:00 p.m. Bakers, delicatessens, and newspaper shops open earlier; flower shops, cake shops, and liquor stores close later. Many shops close later in the evening, especially those located in shopping centers with supermarkets, because many of these have extended hours. Some are open until midnight; others are open twenty-four hours. Banks are usually open from 9:30 a.m. until 4:30 or 5:00 p.m., and there is a move toward banks opening on Saturday mornings.

Supermarkets have replaced most corner shops. Many more are located in vast, one-stop shopping centers alongside all the traditional shops and department stores, cinemas, restaurants, other food outlets (especially the multi-cuisine food halls discussed in Chapter 6), government departments such as Medicare (government medical fund), post offices, and gas stations. In the huge parking garages attached to these shopping centers, take a careful note of exactly where you have parked, identifying your space or the area by level, color, or number.

TV AND RADIO

Many Australians watch a lot of television—children particularly, and very young children more particularly. Many mothers will confess to using the TV as a babysitter, usually in the late afternoon when they are busy preparing the evening meal. The ABC (Australian Broadcasting Commission) caters to this by showing some very good programs, educational as well as entertaining, for children at these times. Adults vary in their viewing, from those who have the TV on in the kitchen-dining area, to those who restrict it to the family room. Many people subscribe to cable TV, and most have VCRs and/or DVDs.

Of interest to you as a visitor or new arrival is Channel SBS (Special Broadcasting Services), which describes itself as: "the voice and vision of multicultural Australia." It is—broadcasting the most comprehensive world news in English every night, and some foreign language news and current affairs programs during the day. Of added value to visitors from overseas (as well as locals) are current affairs programs such as "Dateline" and "Insight."

The daily newspapers give details of programs and times.

The majority of homes now have a computer, which is taking over some of the time school-age children used to spend on watching TV.

There is a quantity of "talk," or "talkback," radio, in which listeners are invited to call the radio station and give their views on news, politics, or any subject that interests them. These programs have half-hourly news broadcasts, plus interviews with politicians (who recognize talk radio as being very influential in changing voting decisions), medical practitioners, lawyers, doctors, teachers, and all experts in their fields. In this way visitors and new arrivals can learn what interests or concerns some Australians—if they can put up with the chatter!

MAKING FRIENDS

First, you have to meet them! Australians are to be found in pubs and clubs, in casual coffee shops, on the beach, at sporting events, at work, and in the variety of other places people might gather.

WHERE TO FIND THEM

Pubs

A pub may also be called a "hotel," or even "the local" (as in "meet you at the hotel," "see you in the pub," "let's try the local"), and may also be referred to as the "local watering hole." Some of the city pubs and a few suburban pubs are quite good, offering reasonably attractive bars, bistros for a meal, and beer gardens for outside eating and drinking. (Children are allowed into beer gardens, but not into the bars.) Beer gardens with bistros are also good "getting together" places in the afternoons and on warm evenings—to meet old friends and to find new ones.

Seek out the pubs that have entertainment—

comedians, bands, singers, and the like. They are good fun, and good places to observe and meet the locals. Melbourne is particularly well known for its comedy scene entertainment in pubs.

Some other pubs are not so attractive, with noise from the TAB (Totaliser Agency Board, which enables betting on most sports) drowning the conversation. Customers combine drinking with betting on the horse races, listening to the race broadcast, and shouting encouragement to horses and jockeys. These places lack the character of many pubs in the U.K.

Beachside pubs can be very rowdy, but offer entertainment and a good time, especially on hot weekends. Look in the entertainment sections of the newspapers on Fridays and at weekends for announcements of times and places.

Every city has quieter, more sophisticated pubs downtown, in which it is possible to sit in comfortable surroundings, often with a city or harbor view, and where you will pay a little more for a relaxing drink or two.

Women go to the better bars, particularly in the city, in groups, or alone. A woman on her own should be prepared to fend off lonely men.

Cafés and Bars
There are plenty of informal cafés and bars in towns, the cafés often serving alcohol as well as

the bars. There are café/bar precincts, such as Darlinghurst in Sydney, and Brunswick Street in Melbourne. Cafés and bars are relaxed and friendly, welcome both sexes, and are very popular with all age ranges, but particularly younger professional people.

Clubs

Mostly in New South Wales—these you must see! Many of these were established by sporting clubs (principally rugby league—see Chapter 5, A God Named Sport) or branches of the RSL (Returned Soldiers League—see Chapter 6, Time Out). They have big, opulent buildings surrounded by lawn bowling greens and filled with poker machines (slot machines), bars, restaurants, gymnasiums, cinemas, and auditoriums for entertainment. They are nonprofit organizations, and because of this are able to offer all their services cheaply— very cheaply. Substantial hot meals, such as roast meats with vegetables, fish and chips, or pasta dishes, can cost under $10. As a visitor to Australia, you will be admitted to any club free (carry some sort of identification), or you must live a certain distance, such as three miles (five kilometers) from the club. You fill in a form at the door. If you are staying in Australia for some time you can take out an annual membership, which varies from $10 to $20.

There are also numerous "ethnic" clubs, for Greeks, Italians, Hungarians, Germans, and so on. While joining a local Australian club carries the advantage of mixing with the locals, if you feel lonely you can mix with locals of your own ethnic background by joining one of these. Look in the telephone directory or on the Internet.

Joining/Avoiding Clubs

It is handy to have one or two club memberships: perhaps a Leagues (rugby) club and an RSL club. Membership entitles you to entry to those clubs anywhere in New South Wales, without the need to prove that you are a visitor to Australia. $30 or $40 at most will get you both, and enable you to enjoy cheap meals and drinks (cheaper than at pubs) wherever you may be, in generally pleasant surroundings, and in good company. At your home club you are also buying the cheapest of gymnasiums, *à la carte* restaurant dining (not as cheap as the club bistro, but still great value), and the opportunity to join in a variety of sports.

Then why avoid them? Well, it is important to be aware that the poker machines (slot machines) subsidize everything in the club. They can be very tempting for visitors, as some of the prizes (such as automobiles) are quite staggering. Suffice it to say that poker machine gambling is a serious problem for some patrons. Each state has its casinos, with poker machines, and they take huge amounts of money daily, even hourly. It is known that New South Wales club poker machines take a big slice of the gambling cake (Australian total gambling turnover exceeds $28 million). So enjoy the clubs, but beware of the "pokies."

Eating Places
There are many casual eating places in shopping centers and tourist areas. They provide a great variety of cuisines for large numbers of people, and you often share a table with others.

Beaches
The wonderful beaches offer much to visitors and locals alike, and tend to be packed, particularly on hot weekends. Visitors need to be careful when swimming or surfing. Stick to the rules (see Chapter 7, Traveling). Apart from swimming, most beaches offer hotels, restaurants with a view, pleasant walks, street shopping, take-out food outlets, and picnic places in parks or on lawns.

Churches
The established Christian churches offer immediate contact with people having similar interests. Or you can join one of the newer and increasingly popular evangelical churches, which are especially popular with Asians. (In these you

will find instant recognition as a newcomer, and a warm welcome. The congregations in the established churches might be a little slower to approach you, but eventually they will.) Similarly, mosques, synagogues, and temples for Hindus, Buddhists, and others are welcoming and offer friendship to new arrivals.

Sporting Events

All sporting events gather crowds—golf, tennis, racing, cricket, and, most of all, football—rugby and "Aussie Rules" (see Chapter 5, A God Named Sport). On a sunny day the atmosphere is bright and happy, and the spectators are well behaved. Bringing your own beer is often not allowed, but you can buy it at the ground. Fans around you will be only too happy to explain the rules.

The Workplace

If you are working in Australia you will, of course, have coworkers. It is common for Aussies to socialize around the coffee machine, at lunch, and after work in a favorite pub.

WHAT NEXT?

So, given these opportunities to meet Australians (and there are no doubt other opportunities), what do you do about it?

First, do not hesitate to introduce yourself.
Aussies generally like the American approach of
an outstretched hand and your name, rather than
the more diffident British approach of standing
back and waiting to be introduced to people
before beginning a conversation. In the work
environment, or at a social function, or at a party
in a friend's house, you are likely to be thought
aloof or snobbish if you wait for an introduction.

Outside the work environment this is obviously
more difficult, especially for women. But men to
men and women to women, it is seen as quite
natural to speak to someone (one, not more—if
there is a group it will be seen as intrusive) with
whom you are sharing a table, or you are sitting
next to at a bar or at a football game. Make a
remark about the food, the view, or anything else
that strikes you, and you will quickly discover if
there is an opportunity for further conversation.
Most people cannot resist a plea for help, so
asking for advice or directions will almost
certainly get you a response.

Becoming a "Mate"
As outlined in Chapter 2, "mateship" was the kind
of fellow-feeling that usually grew out of a shared
experience of adversity, and could not be forced.
In modern Australia there are not quite the same
kinds of adversity to bring people together in

mateship. As we have seen, wives or husbands, as well as bosses, the taxation office, and the police, could provide the adversity, and sticking by your friend through his or her troubles could be the foundation for a new kind of mateship.

But if, when you make friends, you learn about, or at least take an interest in, the interests of your new friends— whether it be home decorating, rugby, early Australian art, gardening, motor bike racing, or anything else—and share your interest with them, then you are on the right path. The next step is to join in—and actively share your common interest.

Shouting a Round

An old Australian saying had it that the worst thing you could do to a man was to steal his beer. Not his wife, or his tucker (food), or his horse, or his good name—but his *beer*.

There is a carry-over into today's culture, when Australians in a group at a bar take turns buying the next round of drinks. It is called "shouting." The term probably comes from early times, when bars were very noisy places and you had to shout to get the barman's attention. To miss out on your shout—

by going to the toilet, or suddenly remembering that you are supposed to be somewhere else, and leaving—means the end of your reputation.

Note for golfers: if you get a hole in one, then at the nineteenth hole—the club bar—you are obliged to shout a drink for everyone who is at the bar!

While something similar to "shouting" might apply in other countries, particularly in the U.K., or sometimes in the U.S.A., there are differences. Firstly it is never questioned in Australia. There is never any doubt about shouting, and whose shout it is. Secondly, shouting transcends rank and wealth. The boss joins in and takes his turn, as does the wealthiest man in the group, as does the one who doesn't have a lot of money.

As a visitor or new arrival, you will earn great respect if you step up early to the bar and say, "It's my shout," because you will be showing an understanding of and respect for a fine old Australian tradition. Keep acting that way, and you could easily find yourself in a situation of becoming a mate.

Receiving Invitations

Australians are great "party animals." They might invite you to all kinds of events or functions—sporting, business, or family. They like to invite people to things they enjoy, and to share their enjoyment—it makes for more fun to have numbers involved. Going to a football game, to a club for a meal and a few beers, simply going down to the "local" on Saturday afternoon, or having a Sunday "barbie," are all much more enjoyable if they can invite someone or, better still, a number of people.

Your chances of being asked along to watch a sporting event depend very much on your having shown, in conversation, an appreciation and knowledge of that particular sport. If you happen to play it yourself, so much the better. Let them see you are an enthusiast. The point is made in Chapter 5, A God Named Sport, that Australians love their sport, and they also love sharing it, either watching or playing, with other people of like mind.

Australians are good at return invitations, which will come as a result of your having invited *them* to something (see below). Don't forget that, when you are invited to an Australian home for a meal, you should take a bottle of reasonably good wine along as a gift.

Some Australians like the idea of having their friends just dropping in for a drink, and this will often happen on a Saturday afternoon. But not everyone welcomes this, so it would be sensible to check with friends rather than make a mistake. If you do drop in, take them something to drink.

And If You Don't Drink Alcohol?

If you don't drink alcohol, just politely refuse
when it is offered. "Actually I don't drink," is fine,
or "Could I have something soft (nonalcoholic),
please?" Australians may feel a bit sorry for you if
you don't drink alcohol, and when they get to
know you better they might say so; but they won't
think poorly of you because of it. It will be quite
generally accepted.

Entertaining

This should not be too much of a problem.
Australians like to go out, and will be flattered
that you ask them. Of course, your arrangements
will vary according to your own circumstances. If
you are living in a house or apartment it will be
easy and natural to invite people to a dinner party
or barbecue there.

Otherwise, you can invite them to come to
your club, or simply to meet you in a
bar or beer garden where they can
join you for a meal. In this case it will
not be expected that you will pay the
bill for everything. If it is your
birthday, or a similar celebration,
you might "shout" a few bottles of
"bubbly" (champagne). If you have
joined an "ethnic" club, it would be a good idea to
invite a friend or friends there—most Australians

will not have been to one before and it will be an adventure for them.

At a formal dinner party you should supply the drink, although guests will usually bring a bottle of wine. You will need some beer, some hard liquor (scotch/gin/vodka) and mixers, and red and white wines. Your guests will be aware of the costs involved for you, and you can expect your invitation to be reciprocated by most of them.

For an informal meal or barbecue, beer and wine will usually be enough, but you may like to start off with an offer of gin and tonic. You supply the food—usually steak, chops, sausages, and salad. If your cooking is up to it, try something like marinated chicken wings, prawns, or lobster.

Invitations should be given at least one week in advance, or two weeks for a formal meal. Verbal invitations are fine.

A GOD NAMED SPORT

Australians often appear to be very laid back, taking adversity and success in their stride. The two most famous Aussie catch phrases, "She'll be right" (everything will be fine), and "No worries" ("don't worry about it"), embrace the essence of the Spanish "*mañana*." But in one area they are very serious: sport.

This might be seen, mistakenly, as indicating that Australians don't work hard, or that they allow sport to interfere with work. Apart from being unwilling to attend Sunday breakfast meetings, there is another tradition: if there is to be a Friday meeting of, say, sales representatives, the first half-hour or so will be given over to a discussion of the upcoming Saturday games. In Melbourne, where the following of the local game, Australian Rules football, is nothing less than fanatical, this could take more like an hour, and many sales managers start their meetings an hour early to allow for it. There is a work ethic and there is a leisure ethic. The following is about the leisure ethic—mostly sports.

Australians draw a sharp distinction between work time and play time, and their favorite form of play is sport, whether as a spectator or a participant. Your surest way to acceptance is through being able to converse about sport, and of course it will help if you become involved in playing—there are always opportunities for tennis, golf, riding, or swimming. It is not difficult to pick up local and international sports knowledge—acres of newsprint and hours of TV are devoted to it. An article about a key sportsman or sportswoman taking drugs, or having an affair with a teammate's wife or husband, will drive the war reports from the front page. Politicians scramble to be associated with sport. Prime Minister John Howard is often seen on television as a serious supporter of cricket.

"Why are the Aussies so good at sport?" is an interesting question. At the Sydney Olympics, compared with the giant populations of the U.S.A. (97 medals), Russia (88 medals), and China (59 medals), Australia, with a tiny population, collected 58 medals. Its record in world rugby, cricket, golf, tennis, swimming, sailing, and hockey, even soccer—the list goes on—is significant in any estimation.

THE CLIMATE AND THE GREAT OUTDOORS

At the level of "weekend" sport, some of the reasons for the general Aussie competence at sport are obvious. Climate plays a huge part in sporting life. Winters being generally short and mild, many ground sports can be played almost all year round. Many schools and homes, whether town or country, have swimming pools; and 80

percent of the population lives within around 30 miles (50 km) of the coast and the beaches. No wonder that many children are brought up swimming, surfing, sailing, surfboarding, windsurfing, water-skiing, and rowing. These leisure activities often turn to sport as the children grow. Many parents find themselves acting as taxidrivers on Saturdays, driving the kids to their sports sessions.

Schools and some churches promote rivalry in sport. Local Councils and Districts promote sport. RSL and other clubs promote sport. There are sports facilities everywhere you look. Drive through the suburbs, or any country town, and you will see just how much of the land is given over to tennis courts, bowling lawns, cricket pitches, and all kinds of other sports grounds, centers, and facilities.

Aside from sport, Australians just like to be outdoors on weekends—going hiking, or more strenuous bush walking; sunbathing on the beach; or simply having a barbecue down on the shore or up in the hills.

THE OLYMPICS AND THE WORLD SCENE
This does not, however, really explain the success of Australians at Olympic and other international sports levels. Growing up with sport can be a precursor to success on the world scene, but few make it. In Australia more make it, *per capita*, than in any other country in the world (if we discount those magnificent individual medal wins by lone athletes from tiny countries). A look at some sporting history might cast some light on the reasons, and will help you, the visitor, to relate to Australia.

Cricket
Cricket is strongly associated with the British (but is believed by some to have been invented by the French). It was played in Australia in the early 1800s. If you do not come from a cricket-playing nation, I suggest that you read up about what can be a most puzzling game.

The first Australian cricket team sent to play in England, in the 1800s, was an all-Aboriginal team. The Melbourne Cricket Club was established in 1838, and the first Test match between English and Australian cricketers was played at the Melbourne Cricket Ground (the MCG—now equally famous as the spiritual home of Australian Rules Football—see below), in 1876. After that match there was talk of a Test Trophy to commemorate England's loss. It was during the next series in Australia that a ball, or the stumps—the three wooden sticks hit into the ground at each end of the pitch—were burnt and the ashes saved in an urn, to be played for as a trophy ever since. These are the "Ashes."

Acknowledged by even the British to be the greatest cricketer of all time, the legendary Sir Donald Bradman (1908–2001) remains one of the great Aussie icons.

But even the "gentleman's game" (the expression "not cricket" means not fair, or not honest), has not escaped controversy. To be a party to any discussion of cricket, at home or in the bar, you need to be aware of two infamous incidents. The first of these is the "bodyline" incident of 1932-3, when the England captain instructed the bowler to bowl directly at Bradman's body in a manner likely to cause injury. Several Aussie batsmen were injured during this tour, and the anti-British feelings of Australians rose to fever pitch.

In the second incident, in 1981, Australia perpetrated the infamy. In a game against New Zealand, another traditional sporting foe, the NZ team, known as the Kiwis, needed six runs to win, with one ball to go—a difficult task, but not impossible. (A hit over the boundary earns six runs.) But it can only be done from traditional bowling, playing a fast ball. The Australian skipper, Greg Chappell, instructed the bowler, his brother Trevor, to bowl the last ball underarm, denying New Zealand the chance to hit a six. Shock! Horror! Australia's reputation for sportsmanship suffered, and underarm bowling was banned, being "underhand" and "not cricket."

Australian Rules Football, and Rugby
"Australian Rules" seems to the uninitiated to be a combination of rugby and soccer, but derives in fact from Gaelic football, as played in Ireland, but adjusted to Australian conditions. Aussie Rules, played in all states, is an authentic item of Australiana: its adherents, who have the fervor of the early Christians, would die in support of their team. They claim, with some validity, that this is the best spectator football game in the world.

In support of this, some years ago, when the two Melbourne teams with the most supporters, Collingwood and Carlton, were due to play the Grand Final at the MCG on the following Saturday, sixty thousand fans braved a wet winter's Thursday night just to watch the Collingwood team practice. In those days the MCG had grandstands and standing room and held some 118,000 spectators for the Grand Finals. Today the oval has seating room only, for about 80,000—soon to be 100,000. An average of 60,000 spectators attend a weekend club game.

The New South Wales supporters call their rugby "the game played in heaven." To Melbourne supporters of Aussie Rules, the MCG *is* "heaven."

Rugby is, of course, international; Aussie Rules is not. Two forms of rugby are played across Australia—Rugby Union (the old game, invented at Rugby School, England) and Rugby League (with changes in rules said to make it more exciting to watch). Rugby club games do not have the spectator support Aussie Rules does, yet Interstate and International games fill the stadiums.

Tennis and Golf
Australia has produced more than its share of tennis greats. The Australian team claimed the Davis Cup, the most prestigious team-tennis

event in the world, twenty times between 1939 and 2000. Some forty Wimbledon winners came from Australia, and the history of the sport could not be told without including the names of Lew Hoad, Ken Rosewall, Rod Laver, Margaret Court, John Newcombe, Evonne Goolagong Cawley, Pat Cash, Pat Rafter, and Leyton Hewitt.

Golf is not the preserve of a moneyed elite, as it is in so many parts of the world, but can be enjoyed by all. As well as some fine private golf courses open to members' guests, there are many public courses. Greg Norman (the Great White Shark) is perhaps Australia's best-known male golfer, as world champion for a number of years, and Carrie Webb the best-known female, also a world champion.

Skiing

The existence of extensive world-class ski-fields comes as a surprise to some visitors. Many Australians and visitors ski in the ski-fields in the highlands between Sydney and Melbourne. The season is generally June to September. Check with a travel agent for transport, accommodation, ski rental, and ski lift passes.

THE MELBOURNE CUP

Australia stops at 3:20 p.m. on the first Tuesday in September. A hush settles over the land from the Northern Territory to Tasmania, while one of the great horse races of the world is run. The first Melbourne Cup was run in 1861, over a distance of 2 miles. When the metric system was adopted, in 1972, it was shortened to 3.2 kilometers.

The preferred method of betting on the Cup (millions of people who would otherwise never place a bet do so on this race), is in the office "sweep," or pool. You will certainly be invited to participate. Everybody puts in, say, $5, and the names of all the horses are drawn randomly from a hat against the names of each member of staff. This eliminates the need to know anything about horse racing— but requires that time be taken off to watch the race. Work stops, across the nation. The entire pot (all the money) is divided appropriately amongst the winner and the two runners-up.

Boats

This is another Australian passion. There are big and small boats—and big and small yachtsmen (kids can be seen skidding around Sydney Harbour and other waterways in tiny single or multihull yachts). It is estimated that there are some 180,000 yachtsmen and over 100,000 speedboat owners in Australia. Australia has competed in the prestigious sailing event The America's Cup (named not after the country but the first winner, the yacht *America*) since 1962. In 1983 Australia, with the yacht *Australia II*, became the first nation to take the cup away from America since the inaugural race in 1851.

A LAND OF OPPORTUNITY

So Australians live in a land of sporting opportunity, with the climate, the proximity of the beaches, and the wide-open spaces all contributing to sporting endeavor. They often take up sports while very young, playing one form in winter and often more than one in summer, at school, then for the District or Club, for the State, and then, of course, some for their country. Why do they do so well internationally?

Anyone who has achieved success at a national level and beyond will tell you that it takes more than natural ability, early experience, training, and practice. To start training before dawn and finish in the dark all year round; to diet and exercise continually; to forgo most social life; to struggle to improve one's performance, and to hurt, strain, and torture tired muscles—all these and more require something else.

The Aboriginal peoples have supplied some of Australia's best sportsmen and women. Also, from the time of their arrival, the Australian settlers set out with something to prove. They had to conquer a harsh land and overcome the disadvantages of arriving with little, in many cases nothing. They were looked down on as convicts, or at best as colonials. They needed to succeed.

All this applied in sport as well as in life; in fact, in the beginning, there was only work and sport. Some were driven more than others—and were more successful than others—but they set the benchmark and then raised it higher and higher, pulling the rest up with them. There can be no doubt that high standards, and the adulation of their young compatriots to those who set them, have contributed to an intense desire to emulate these sporting heroes.

Massive media coverage of these men and women and their achievements provides an irresistible challenge to many young people. Success breeds success. As a result, many Australian adults play and enjoy a social game; many participate in competitive matches; some give their all in major events; and the heroes are international conquerors.

Not all Australians are active sportsmen and women. As a visitor you will not automatically be expected to have sporting accomplishments: it is understood not to be within everybody's ability. Australians, particularly those who have children who do not shine at sport, who prefer studying, or reading, or using their computers, do not have unrealistic sporting expectations; but they do have, and share, interest in achievements in one sport or another. You will be comfortably accepted into Australian society at any level if you can join in discussions on sport and sporting achievements both in Australia and in your own country. If you talk about your country's successes, expect some good-natured banter. Any suggestion that another country is good at sport will be irresistible to the Aussie sense of humor. But you can also expect respect for your interest and knowledge.

chapter six

TIME OUT

FOOD AND DRINK

Thanks to the Greek god Dionysus, and the
Roman Bacchus, for the changes the Greeks and
Italians made to Australian cuisine (at that time
really an oxymoron) from the 1950s. Thanks to all
the later immigrants who brought with them their
wonderful varieties of food and cooking styles,
and set Australians on the path to wine
appreciation. And thanks to the Germans,
Lebanese, Vietnamese, Indonesians, Indians,
French, Thais, Chinese, Yugoslavs, Africans,
Japanese, Hungarians, and all those many others
who have contributed to what has now perhaps
become the most tantalizing and varied
international cuisine in the world.

Fresh Food

Australia's great varieties of climate, from the
tropics in the north, through irrigated plains and
mountains, to coasts with Mediterranean
climates, mean that a multitude of fresh
ingredients are readily available—from paw-paw

(papaya), bananas, pineapples, avocados, and mangoes in the north to nectarines, peaches, apricots, strawberries, raspberries, and apples in the south. Immigrants have given Australia lemongrass, eggplant (aubergine), zucchini, garlic, basil, coriander, artichoke, bok choy, shiitake mushroom, and on and on and on—all fresh daily in your local supermarket or vegetable market.

Australian beef is good enough to be exported to the U.S.A. The lamb is nearly as good as New Zealand lamb. The pork is rich (and a little fatty, which gives it taste, unlike much European pork).

And the fish! Because of the length of Australia's coastline, from warm tropical waters off the Queensland coast to cold waters off southern Australia, you can sample barramundi, mud crabs, and coral trout from the north; prawns and world-famous oysters from New South Wales, Tasmania, and South Australia; deep-sea whiting, crayfish, lobster, and cultivated Atlantic salmon in the south.

Glossary of Food Terms

Anzac biscuits
Biscuits made from rolled oats and honey. As sent to the Anzac troops at Gallipoli during World War I.

Balmain bugs (and Moreton Bay Bugs)
A type of small, saltwater crayfish.

Chiko rolls
Deep-fried rolls filled with savory vegetables.

Damper
A flat bread made with flour and water and baked in the embers of a fire.

Finger buns
Long, narrow yeast buns covered with pink icing.

Floater
A meat pie floating in green pea soup.

Lamington
A sponge cake, covered with a thin layer of chocolate and desiccated coconut.

Pavlova
A meringue base piled high with fruit and cream, named after the lightness of the famous ballerina.

Sausage rolls
Sausage meat wrapped in pastry.

Vegemite
Australia's most famous and much loved spread, made from yeast extract.

Violet Crumble Bar
Made by Hoadleys, a revered confection made from honeycomb covered with chocolate.

Yabbies
Small, freshwater crayfish.

It is difficult not to be enthusiastic about the food in Australia. But it gets even better . . .

Wines

Although beer is still the most widely consumed beverage by volume, Australia is rapidly becoming a wine-drinking nation. It produces some of the best wine in the world, exporting 50 percent of production, selling more wine in the U.K. than in any other country, and actually selling wine to France! Wine is very reasonably priced if you buy carefully (see below for advice). And there is BYO!

For any wine-loving visitor, an hour's drive from most capital cities will have you sitting in a cellar-door tasting room, sipping some of the world's finest wine. Many of these vineyards have restaurants, and many can be visited as part of a conducted wine tour. Most can also be reached by bus or train—not a bad idea because of Australia's drinking and driving regulations (a blood alcohol level of over .05 percent could lead to a fine and loss of driver's license)—although once at the wine-growing area it will then be hard to get around.

The advantage of a tour is that most of the approximately 1,500 vineyards are clustered in distinct regions, and it is relatively easy to make visits to different vineyards and be back in the city for dinner. Examples of these are the Mornington Peninsula, south of Melbourne; McLaren Vale, south of Adelaide; and Margaret River, south of Perth. The Hunter Valley, north of Sydney, is the closest to that city. You can pick up free brochures with descriptions of individual wineries from the state tourist offices.

Over half of the total wine production comes from what is known as the Riverland, a region irrigated by two of Australia's largest rivers, the Murray and the Darling, which merge near the borders of New South Wales, Victoria, and South Australia. Much of the wine grown in these areas is sold domestically in an Australian invention, the cardboard wine cask—wine in a box. The wine is sealed in an aluminum foil or plastic bladder—you can draw by the glass from the tap—which seals the wine from the air. It will keep for days, even a week or so.

Australians are extremely fond of their "Chateau Cardboard" (this is often as good as bottled wine, and is the result of oversupply at the vineyard), however it is usually consumed informally at home. Social convention dictates that bottles of wine are opened for visitors and at dinner parties—and you are judged by your choice of wine. Remember, too, that it is polite to open wine brought by a guest.

BYO—BRING YOUR OWN

This concept, which is very common in Australia, means that you can take your own wine to many restaurants. Imagine the savings! Buy your wine at a good price in one of the many bottle shops you will find dotted around cities and suburbs (somewhat similar to U.S. liquor stores and U.K. off licenses, they offer a very wide choice of wines)—and take it to the restaurant you fancy.

You should note that most restaurants that accept BYO will state the fact in the window, on the menu, and in their advertisements. Others that have liquor licenses will allow you to bring your wine and will supply glasses, but will charge you corkage—perhaps fifty cents to two or three dollars a bottle, or fifty cents for each drinker. Even so, you will save considerably by buying at a bottle shop. Note that BYO applies to bottles of wine only, not casks!

A few elite and middle-range restaurants do not allow BYO, and it is advisable to enquire before making a reservation. Then you can decide whether or not you wish to pay the extra for what might well be superior food and drink.

Buying Wines

1. Price is a guide to quality, but it is also advisable to read the wine reviews in newspapers for tips on the good wines currently available. Buy from major liquor outlets rather than from pubs/hotels.

2. Perfectly acceptable wine to take to friends can be bought for under $15 a bottle. For yourself, if you want to spend less, perhaps $8-plus.

3. Very good wines probably cost over $15 a bottle, exceptional wines over $30.

4. As the roughest of guides to grape and district, try the following. (Australian labels are tightly controlled by the Trade Practices Act. Labels accurately describe origin, contents, year, and alcoholic content—and you can read the label.)

Red Wines

Shiraz (claret from the Rhône) from McLaren Vale, Barossa Valley, or Central Victoria.

Cabernet Sauvignon (the great grape of Bordeaux) from Coonawarra, Barossa Valley, or Margaret River.

Cabernet/Shiraz from any of the above areas.

Merlot from BarossaValley, McLaren Vale, or Central Victoria.

Pinot Noir (original grape from Burgundy) from Tasmania, Yarra Valley, or Mornington Peninsula.

White Wines

Chardonnay from anywhere—said to be "a
    promiscuous grape—grows anywhere."
Riesling (originally Rhine Riesling) from the
    Clare Valley, Coonawarra, Tasmania.
Semillon (a Bordeaux grape) from the Hunter
    Valley (must be a few years old); or South
    Australia or Goulburn Valley (to drink now).
If you have a real interest in wines, and you have
not been to New Zealand, try some of their white
wines from Cloudy Bay or the Marlborough
region, readily available in Australia.

Casks

"Chateau Cardboard" comes mostly in 2-liter and
4-liter casks packaged by some of the best-known
vineyards. The 2-liter casks are generally, but not
always, of higher quality.

Some good-value red wine buys are: Yalumba
2-liter Merlot; Lindeman 4-liter Premium Variety
Shiraz; and Cabernet Morris 4-liter "pressings."

Good-value whites: Lindeman 4-liter Premium
Varietal Chardonnay; Morris 4-liter Reserve
Chardonnay; Morris 4-liter Premium Dry White.

RESTAURANTS

As has been said, Australia offers perhaps the
greatest variety of ethnic cuisines anywhere in the

world, from Moroccan to Chinese in its many forms—the ubiquitous Chinese restaurants are today the purveyors of Cantonese, Pekingese, Szechuan (Szechwan), Hakka, and Shanghai food, cooked by people from the place of origin. Many city and suburban shopping centers, and other locations such as Darling Harbour in Sydney, have this wide variety, offered from many small outlets, side by side.

The introduction of these ethnic styles has prompted the rise of what is known as Modern Australian cuisine—multiculturalism on the table. Master chefs, often with French flair and Asian overtones, create combinations of fresh ingredients in new and imaginative ways.

Special Occasion?

If you decide to eat out in an expensive restaurant, it might be best to go on a Friday, Thursday, or Wednesday night—in that order of preference. A Saturday night is likely to be busier, noisier, and less relaxing.

TABLE MANNERS

Table manners generally follow the British tradition. If the food does not need to be cut with a knife, it is quite correct just to use a fork in the right hand; but otherwise Australians do not cut up their food and then put the knife down and eat with a fork in the American way. The knife should be held (with the handle covered by your hand, not like a pencil), while the fork (facing down) lifts the food. It is polite to put them both down on the plate while you chew your mouthful.

At the end of the course the knife and fork are placed together in the center of the plate, with the fork facing upward, so that the waiter or your hostess will know that you have finished eating; but the table will be cleared only when everyone has finished. Knife and fork laid separately on a plate on which there is still some food indicates to the waiter that you have not finished.

In a Chinese restaurant, most Australians use chopsticks. Practice does make perfect, and any Chinese waiter will be only too happy to demonstrate. But don't be embarrassed to ask for a fork and spoon. The usual custom in Australia is for everyone at the table to choose a dish, and then share the food. If you use chopsticks, and particularly if you are with Chinese people, etiquette requires that you should use a spoon to take food from a shared dish to your plate or bowl, and not dip your chopsticks into the communal food. It is good manners to eat some rice before you select other food, so that you are not then overly hungry.

With Western cuisine it is customary for women to be asked first for their choice, and quite common for the man to ask this before the waiter arrives and for him to order for both. The bill for a group of people is usually divided and shared, singles paying their single share (and this usually includes single women in a mixed group) and the couple paying double.

As a visitor you may well be encouraged by a tour guide, or some restaurateurs, to try some kind of "bush tucker." Interest in this has grown recently, since new Australians have come to appreciate that Aborigines survived healthily on local food for centuries before white man's food was introduced—in the very early days this was all imported.

You might be offered witchetty grubs, either cooked or raw and live. These are the larvae of wood-boring moths found in holes in tree trunks, and visitors find them fascinating in a way that is certainly not shared by most locals. If you do accept an offer to try this delicacy (or another, the honey ant—a fat ant which stores a honeylike substance in its abdomen), remember to hold them by the head and eat the rest, or bite the head off first.

Kangaroo, buffalo, camel, crocodile, wild turkey, and other delicacies are also finding their way on to some restaurant menus.

It is worth noting that in restaurants the word "entrée" means the starter, or first course, and if cheese is to be served it will be as a separate course, and sometimes before the dessert (often referred to as "sweets").

TIPPING

Perhaps because of the egalitarian spirit in Australia, tipping is not the problem it can be in other countries. Australians tend to feel that a waiter or waitress should earn a tip through extra or very friendly service. Given that, they are recognized as not being well paid and most Australians will "share the wealth" (pass on some of their money to help another) by paying a little more than the bill requires. Typically private individuals tip 10 to 15 percent, and businessmen 15 percent. GST (Goods and Services Tax) of 10 percent will be shown on the bill.

THE "BARBIE," OR "BAR-B-QUE"

Not much needs to be said about a "barbie." The old typical party scenario, in which the guys stayed around the beer keg or esky (cold bottle carrier) while the women sat and talked about their babies, is thankfully long gone. However, there is often a preliminary scene when the guys gather to offer cooking advice and have the first tinnie (can of beer). The constant turning method often practiced allows most of the juices to drip away, leaving the meat dry and tough.

Australians are protective of their barbies, but should you, the visitor, be asked to lend a hand, you should know that meat should be turned only twice. First place it on one side for just a minute to seal in the juices, and then turn on to the other side for about eight minutes (for steak), then back to the first side for a further six or seven minutes. This applies to both open grill and hotplate. Some say that good steak should if possible be cooked on the hotplate first, and then briefly over the open-flame grill just to crisp the edges. You will be hailed as a star if you get it right.

When you are invited to a barbecue, it is customary to ask if you can bring some meat. In fact (except among close friends) this offer is usually refused. But do take a bottle of wine.

SANGERS AND OTHER TAKEAWAYS

Australians are much given to diminutives (see Chapter 9, Communicating), such as "sangers," or "sannies," for "sandwiches." The common sandwich, still standard fare for blue and white collar workers, these days has amazing fillings and salads piled high as a result of Western influence. It has therefore grown in size and, in some cases, elegance. There is almost nothing that cannot be put in a sanger, these days. Now it is also often "open," that is, only one slice of bread or roll is used, layered with a variety of salads—very attractive, and very healthy.

One of the less fortunate types of food import has been American-style fast food. Overeating of Kentucky Fried Chicken, McDonald's burgers and French fries, and the like, has brought about a weight revolution, and many Australians have joined their American cousins in their obesity problem. Some 38 percent of Australian adults are now classified as overweight or obese. Recently, however, there has been a backlash, driven mainly by general concern about children growing up unfit and with a "junk-food mentality." As a result, Australians are now becoming more health-food conscious.

For you, the tourist, the deep-fried foods are there—everywhere—if you want them. And you might just try some of the best fish and chips to be had, battered and salted, along with fried calamari, Chinese spring rolls, local chiko rolls, and Indian samousas, or samosas. Walk into the local fish and chip shop, check what is available, and order some take-out.

AUSTRALIAN CULTURE—AN OXYMORON?

Customs and Traditions

If you know little else about Australian customs when you arrive in the country, you will need to know about the tradition of Anzac Day. Wherever you find yourself on April 25—considered by most Australians as their most important holiday—there will be an Anzac Day parade. On this day old and young soldiers march together to the local war memorial, to the accompaniment of a brass band. Many of them will probably be wearing the distinctive Australian slouch hat that has the left side of the brim cocked up to allow a rifle to be swung on to the shoulder. Children join in the parade alongside their soldier fathers and grandfathers. At the war memorial there will be emotional speeches, a minute's silence, and the reverent intonation of Laurence Binyon's "Poem for the Fallen":

> *They shall not grow old, as we that*
>   *are left grow old.*
> *Age shall not weary them, nor the*
>   *years condemn.*
> *At the going down of the sun and in*
>   *the morning,*
> *We will remember them.*

In every RSL (Returned Soldiers League) club across the land, at 6:00 p.m., the poker machines will cease their cacophony and a hush will settle over the people, who turn to face west and offer a minute's silence for those who fell in battle.

Why?

Anzac Day commemorates the enormous sacrifices made by the Anzacs (the Australian and New Zealand Army Corps) in World War I, in the Allied attempt at Gallipoli, in Turkey, to force a way through the Dardanelles and link up with Russia. History confirms that this attempt was doomed from the start. Much of the tragedy lies in the fact that the military commanders, from Winston Churchill down, made a terrible blunder. Thousands were sent out of the trenches and into the teeth of established Turkish machine gun posts, to be shot down, their bodies piling up to be climbed over by the next wave.

Between April 25 and December 19, 1915, over eight thousand Australians and two thousand New Zealanders were killed (two thousand on the first day alone), and nineteen thousand Australians wounded, in a battle on the other side of the world, defending the British Empire.

The bravery of these men in the face of hopeless odds, the nobility of their courage in attempting the impossible, and their legendary mateship unto death, won them a reputation that endures to this day. The Australian director Peter Weir's epic film *Gallipoli* conveys this well. Find a video of it if you can.

The Gay and Lesbian Mardi Gras
Sydney has been called the "gay capital" of the Southern Hemisphere. Sydneysiders are not too sure (and not necessarily too pleased) about that—but it certainly becomes true once a year, in March. In 2003, at least five thousand people and 140 floats wound their way along Oxford Street in Sydney to celebrate twenty-five years of Mardi Gras. Half a million people—"straights"—men, women, and children—whole families—waved and cheered from the sidelines. In an expression of what is, to many older Australians (who were brought up in an era when "queer" bashing, for some, was a game), great tolerance, even the New South Wales police force has a float manned by gay policemen and women.

***Real* Culture—Ballet, Opera, Music, Literature**
Australians have excelled in ballet, despite the country's macho self-image. There are around 2,500 ballet schools in the country, arising from

the examples, traditions, and innovations of dancers such as Sir Robert Helpmann in the 1920s and 1930s; Marilyn Jones in the 1960s; and, more recently, Lisa Bolte, Meryl Tankard, and Graham Murphy.

Australia has produced a number of world-class operatic singers, such as Dame Nellie Melba, in the nineteenth century, Dame Joan Sutherland, John Brownlee, and Peter Dawson in the twentieth. The prestigious Australian Opera was established in 1970.

An important figure in Australian musical development was Sir Bernard Heinze, who in the late 1920s became musical advisor to the Australian Broadcasting Commission. With his knowledge and inspiration he helped to bring a range of high-quality orchestral music to the Australian public. Other famous musical names include the composer Percy Grainger, the concert pianist Eileen Joyce, and the classical guitarist John Williams.

On a lighter musical note, the Bee Gees and the Easy Beats, INXS, Men At Work, Midnight Oil, Little River Band, AC/DC, and the Black Sorrows have all made their mark on the pop world. Two essentially Australian bands are Gondwanaland, blending white and Aboriginal music, and the Aboriginal Yothu Yindi, with a great mix of traditional sound and modern technology.

Then there are the singers and actors Olivia Newton-John and Kylie Minogue, and the younger Natalie Imbruglia, Delta Goodrem, and Holly Valance. The Australian TV soap opera *Neighbours* is viewed around the world, and has provided a platform for the launch of many young actors' careers.

The Australian literary scene will provide the visitor with distinctly Australian voices on singularly Australian themes. Read the following, and you will be better equipped than many of your hosts:

Capricornia and, if you have the time, *Poor Fellow My Country*, by Xavier Herbert.

The Eye of the Storm, and others, by Patrick White.

The Chant of Jimmy Blacksmith, and others, by Thomas Keneally .

An Imaginary Life, by David Malouf.

True History of the Kelly Gang, by Peter Carey.

The Tyranny of Distance, by Geoffrey Blainey.

The Fatal Shore, by Robert Hughes.

The Female Eunuch, by Germaine Greer.

The Lucky Country, by Donald Horne.

The Thorn Birds, by Colleen McCulloch.

A Town Like Alice, by Nevil Shute.

Other Australian writers of note include Miles
Franklin, Christina Stead, Helen Garner, Bryce
Courtney, Elizabeth Jolley, and Tim Winton, and
see the works listed under "Further Reading" at
the end of this book.

Painting

Aboriginal Art, traditionally executed chiefly
using ochre paintings on cave walls, strips of bark,
wood, and their own bodies, has achieved an
international reputation in recent decades.
Rock art is concentrated in northern areas of
Australia, with the largest collection located
in Kakadu National Park and
neighboring Arnhem Land—it is the
most extraordinary collection in the
world. Especially well known are
the dot-mosaic and X-ray styles of
painting, depicting animals with
their skeletal structure and internal
organs. Examples can be seen in all
major public galleries, and can be
readily purchased in galleries and
Aboriginal shops. Artists like Albert Namatjira
transferred their talents to watercolors and oils.

The works of white artists grew away from the
early colonials' depictions of Australian scenes.
The painters S. T. Gill, Tom Roberts, Arthur
Streeton, Fred Williams, and Fred McCubbin are

widely credited with viewing and representing the Australian landscape through Australian, not European eyes.

Styles changed little until the social-realist depictions of immigrants and the working classes by Noel Counihan and Josi Bergner. Sidney Nolan contributed near abstracts of the bushranger (robber) Ned Kelly, and some depictions of famous historical events; William Dobell, portraiture; and Russell Drysdale, stark outback landscapes and lifestyles.

Australian art today is diverse, and is perhaps more modern in its appreciation of the natural environment. Designer Ken Done has added graphics, and Brett Whitley some vibrant explorations of landscapes and domestic situations.

Cinema

Australians made movies before the 1950s. Some were pretty awful—and they still turn out some dross at times. But there are also some giants of the Australian industry: cinematographers like Peter Weir—*Picnic at Hanging Rock* (1975), *Gallipoli* (1981), *Fearless* (1993), *Dead Poet's Society* (1989); Fred Schepesi—*The Chant of Jimmy Blacksmith* (1978); *Six Degrees of Separation* (1993); Bruce Beresford—*The Getting of Wisdom* (1977), *Breaker Morant* (1980), *Driving Miss Daisy* (1990); Gillian Armstrong—

My Brilliant Career (1978), *Little Women* (1995). Other movies of note include *Strictly Ballroom, Mad Max, Crocodile Dundee, Priscilla Queen of the Desert,* and *Lantana.*

Some Australian actors who have gained an international reputation are Nicole Kidman, Toni Collette, Cate Blanchett, Judy Davis, Mel Gibson, Brian Brown, Geoffrey Rush, Rachel Griffiths, Sam Neill, Jack Thomson, Hugo Weaving, and Guy Pearce. And, going back a bit, Merle Oberon and Errol Flynn.

Contemporary Australians are creating a new and vibrant cultural tradition.

chapter seven

TRAVELING

GOING WALKABOUT

It will be obvious to a visitor that there is a lot to
see and do in Australia. While many people tend
to overplan overseas trips, this is one country
where forward planning will greatly improve your
stay. Many visitors want to see the Great Barrier
Reef, Uluru (Ayers Rock), and Bondi Beach in
Sydney, and to have a meal in one of the fine
restaurants of Melbourne.

But Townsville, in Queensland, from where you
can take a plane or boat to the reef just halfway up
the reef's length, is about 850 miles (1,367 km)

from Brisbane, which in turn is nearly the same distance from Sydney. Melbourne is about 540 miles (873 km) from Sydney. Uluru via Alice Springs is over 1,200 miles (nearly 2,000 km) if you are flying from Sydney, but many more (1,820 miles, or 2,931 km) if you are traveling by road.

Wherever you land, which will most likely be in Sydney, Melbourne, or Perth, it is a good idea to give yourself a few days to adjust your body clock—both from jetlag and from differences in seasons, especially if you have arrived from the Northern Hemisphere—before you set out to tackle these vast distances.

The following pages will help you to make your travel plans, to make decisions about destinations, and to select from the almost overwhelming number of choices. They will also help you to understand some of the differences between the Australian states, and the differing attitudes of the Australians who live in them.

PLANNING YOUR TRIP

Going on holiday can be one of the most memorable events of your life. But it can be memorably *good* or memorably *bad*. The fact is that it can become a nightmare if you rely totally on travel agents, brokers, or tour operators.

With access to the Internet, you are now able to

Some Travel Tips

Australia is a very user-friendly country when it comes to travel, but you need to be careful about some things:

Free extras
Nothing is free—you will be paying somewhere.

Package deals
Many claim to be cheap and to save you money. You will get what you have paid for—a low standard.

Hidden extras
Look for things like charges for washing bed linens; key deposits; taxes.

Hostel chains
Some are excellent; many are not.

Discount cards
These generally offer no better deal than you can negotiate yourself.

Credit card numbers
Give these only as a last resort to secure a booking.

Valuables
Store these with Reception, and obtain a receipt.

research, to investigate the environment you plan to be in, and to adjust your plans to take differences and peculiarities into account. You can make bookings for flights, accommodation, tours, and many kinds of goods and services. Even if you do decide to book through a reputable travel agent, you can still do plenty of research and make informed decisions before doing so. The end result will usually be lower prices and the result you want, rather than possibly being persuaded into something you may not like.

If you deal with a travel agent, be sure to tell them exactly what you want. If they recommend certain airlines, accommodation, etc., check prices and alternatives elsewhere. The agent may be working on commission for clients. So shop around before you buy, because prices can vary considerably. Don't make quick decisions—take time to study any quotes before committing yourself. Check that the agent has a reasonable refund policy.

STATE DIFFERENCES AND RIVALRIES

The rivalry between states is largely, but not entirely, in jest, and should be understood by visitors in that light. Sometimes the humor is shared.

An example derives from the fact that the New South Wales police have, over the years, suffered allegations of corruption, and some of these have been corroborated by investigations through a number of Royal Commissions. Visitors should note that the corruption has been internal, and at a high level—heaven help anyone who thinks he can bribe an ordinary policeman during the performance of his duties. Equally, the Victorian police have a reputation for shooting (criminals) first and asking questions later. A favorite story shared by people in both states concerns a big cross-border raid made by police from both states in the 1990s. The NSW police are claimed to have said to the Victorian police, "Look, we won't take anything if you don't shoot anybody."

Sydney, New South Wales, with a population of four million, is the largest city in Australia. It has taken over from its closest rival, Melbourne, as the financial center of the country, and likes to think of itself as the more worldly capital. After all, it has the Gay and Lesbian Mardi Gras, topless beaches, rugby, and the Opera House (as the locals will tell you, often in that order).

Manly and Bondi Beaches are popular favorites with tourists, and Sydneysiders know that they have the best beaches, the best harbor, and the best climate. Of Melbourne, they will say things like: "It's a terrible place. I went there once and it was raining," or, "the best thing to come out of Melbourne is the Hume Highway" (it goes to Sydney). Sydneysiders look down on all other state capitals, but particularly Melbourne.

Melbourne, Victoria, has a population of more than three million. It was the financial center of Australia, and is considered the cultural center, and more "Victorian" (as in Victorian 1890s England) in attitude and style than Sydney. The "Vics" (Victorians) will cheerfully tell you that this is because Melbourne was settled by free settlers, while Sydney was settled by convicts— "and it still shows."

Melbourne is said to be the second-largest Greek city in the world, after Athens. Also, more immigrant Italians stayed in Melbourne than in any other city. This, together with the arrival of other immigrants from elsewhere, has given the city a cosmopolitan variety of restaurants— arguably more so than Sydney.

A good Melbourne story relates a comment made by the American actress Ava Gardner, when she was starring in the movie *On the Beach* in 1959. She was asked what she thought of Melbourne. She said: "Well, the movie is about the end of the world—and they couldn't have found a better place." Today, Melbourne is an elegant city with something of a Parisian flavor—some beautiful buildings on wide, tree-lined streets with open-air dining. Melbournians are justly proud of their art galleries and theaters. As a visitor you will be made very welcome— particularly if you don't tell them that you visited Sydney first. Melbournians look down on all other state capitals and try to ignore Sydney.

Brisbane, Queensland, has a population of more than 1.5 million. Queenslanders have a saying about their state and the climate: "beautiful one day, perfect the next." This will be said to you

with a straight face (and as a visitor, the best
advice is for you to keep a straight face too)—a
face from which they are wiping the beads of
perspiration resulting from high humidity and
high temperatures. They are inordinately proud of
their Gold Coast. The Sunshine coast, where you
will find the town of Noosa, is lush and tropical.
Further north, in fact as far as Port Douglas, the
coast has some beautiful beaches, and interesting
country towns providing ready access to the Great
Barrier Reef.

Queenslanders look down on people from
"south of the border" (with New South Wales),
calling them "Mexicans" (truly). As a visitor, you
can claim you were just "passing through" New
South Wales in order to get to Queensland.

Darwin, on the coast of the Northern Territory,
has a population of 77,000. The remote splendor
of the environment, the relaxed lifestyle, the
multicultural mix, and a younger than average
population give it a distinctively frontier feel.

Adelaide, South Australia, referred to as "the
city of churches," has a population of about one
million. A Colonel Light, who laid it out neatly on
a "square" of nearly equal sides, designed the city.
The settlers were all free, many coming on paid
voyages directly to South Australia, and the place
has a reputation for being rather staid and quiet:
"well laid out and ready to be buried," according

to Sydneysiders and Melbournians. The city is charming, with fine restaurants in tree-lined streets, and a calming pace of life. A travel writer once wrote, "Adelaide is a delightful place to stop—for lunch."

Adelaidians also have a reputation for being snobbish. It is said that, on being introduced to you, they ask not where you come from, what your job is, or how much you earn, but what school you went to. (But although they may look down on folk from all the other states because they didn't go to the "right" school, many of them leave to go to university in other states.)

However, the city belies its staid and stuffy reputation. It has many more hotels per head of population than other capitals; it had topless bars before the other states; and it had an allegedly gay Premier who was supported by the people, who advanced civil rights, and who gave great support to an event of international importance—the Adelaide Festival of the Arts. Nearby is the Barossa Valley, home of some fine Australian wineries, and a delightful area to visit (and sample).

Perth, Western Australia, has a population of over one million. It is the most isolated modern city in the world. This has an effect on the collective psyche of its inhabitants—they are aware that they are isolated, and they are glad of it.

Western Australians ironically call Australians from the eastern seaboard (especially Sydney and Melbourne) "the Wise Men from the East"—a biblical metaphor. Western Australians resent the way Sydneysiders and Melbournians tell them how to run their state. Western Australia, having most of the gold and nickel, and reserves of oil and timber, is, they say, the only financially independent state.

Perth has a warm climate, miles of enticing beaches, and all that money. Perth people are very friendly to anybody who is not from Sydney or Melbourne (South Australians are just acceptable, being also somewhat distant from the "Wise Men"—and it is doubtful if Western Australians can relate at all to Tasmanians or Queenslanders, who are further away, geographically, than Singaporeans). As a visitor from overseas, however, you will be most welcome.

Canberra, Australian Capital Territory, the

Federal Capital and Seat of Government, has a population of more than three hundred thousand. Australians visiting from other cities deny this, claiming that there are actually no people there, just controlled robot figures that drive robot cars at regular intervals around empty buildings. When you visit the city, you will see what they mean. However, Canberra does have a wonderful gardener—it is a very pretty city, especially during the spring flower festival, Floriade. The National Gallery of Australia in Canberra is the best gallery in the country, housing Aboriginal and other Australian art, along with a fine international collection; there is a huge War Memorial, and a distinguished Parliament House. And it is close to Sydney. People from Canberra look down on anybody below Cabinet Secretary level.

Hobart, Tasmania, has a population of over 190,000. The Tasmanians are most welcoming folk, with strong ties to the U.K., and Tasmania is a wonderful place for a relaxing holiday. It also offers the best opportunity you will have to see what the convict days were really like—at Port Arthur. Mainlanders will tell you that the Tasmanians welcome any visitors—for someone to talk to.

The Tasmanians in general do not look much further than their coast, and Tasmania is likewise

sometimes forgotten by the rest of Australia.
Once, at the Commonwealth Games held in
Brisbane, there was an opening display by
schoolchildren, who gathered in the arena
to form a map of Australia—but they forgot to
include Tasmania.

TRANSPORT

Buses

The great majority of Australians live in cities
where urban transport is much the same as any
other metropolitan areas around the world. City
and suburban buses carry commuters and
visitors, as do trains, trams (streetcars, which
operate in Melbourne and Adelaide), and tour
buses. The main tour bus company in Australia is
McCaffertys/Greyhound, which maintains a
country-wide service. There are several other
companies, operating mostly between Sydney,
Melbourne, and Adelaide. The
best way to travel around
Australia by bus is with a
Bus Pass. These
can be based on
distance, or have
a number of
months' validity. Buying

sector fares is more expensive than the Pass,
and should be considered only if you going from
A to B in less than a week. There are some great
tour buses, such as Wayward Bus and Oz
Experience, but they travel only between large
Backpacker resorts.

Trains

Australia has some of the world's great train
journeys. Check out the Indian Pacific (from
Sydney via Adelaide to Perth), the Ghan, named
after Afghan camel trains (from Adelaide to Alice
Springs and soon through to Darwin), and the
Queenslander (from Brisbane to Cairns).

The Indian Pacific covers the longest stretch of
straight rail in the world (over 300 miles, or 500
km, without a bend), and the Ghan covers the
longest north-south rail line in the world.

There is no Australian equivalent of the Euro
Pass (which Aussies can purchase at a discount in
Australia for train travel in Europe). However,
there are many good deals to be had in nearly all
states on passes as well as discount specials.
Remember that Australia is a huge country, and
some of these trips are measured in days rather
than hours.

For state-run trains, call the transport
information number in the state capital, or any
travel agent.

Flying

Qantas and Virgin Blue are the two main airlines within Australia, and both offer special fares for domestic (internal) and international travel. Booking is available, and is often cheaper, on the Internet. Within each state there are regional airlines, which can also offer good deals.

It is a good idea to check with your local travel agent about special international tourist concessions and advice.

Car

There can be no better way to see Australia than by car, camper, or motorcycle. Either renting or buying is straightforward—with some cautions: when purchasing a vehicle it is much safer to buy from a licensed dealer. In Australia a dealer might not be any more or less honest than in your country, but he is governed by consumer protection laws that ensure that there is no "winding back of the clock" (tampering with the odometer), or other malpractice; and that for vehicles over a certain price a warranty must be provided. Becoming a member of a road organization (found through a travel agent or car sales/rental company, or see the list on pages 162–3) entitles you to roadside repairs, towing, and the provision of advice and maps. Be careful of Backpacker companies (see Backpacking, below), which sometimes offer station wagons that have circumnavigated the country more times than you might wish.

All of the above can be explored through your travel agent, or on the Internet (try Google Search, or Alta Vista, or the like: Travel information Australia).

The Law

If you are a foreign visitor intending to drive, you should carry an International Driver's License, obtainable from your home country before you leave. This will entitle you to rent and drive a car in all states.

Each state has its own driving license, and its own local rules. It is obligatory on your part that you know and observe these rules, particularly the speed limits. Local police may be tolerant with foreign visitors about minor breaches, but not about speeding. You can obtain a copy of local driving rules from the government department in charge of roads and traffic in each state—check the telephone book, or ask a local travel agent or the car-rental company.

Drinking and Driving—Don't Do It!

Random breath testing of drivers for alcohol consumption is carried out in all states. You may be stopped and tested by police at any time.

If the police are called to the scene of an accident, they are also likely to carry out a breath test. However slight the accident may be, if a foreign visitor is involved the other driver might well call the police because of doubts about insurance coverage.

The amount of alcohol you can consume before it becomes illegal to drive varies slightly between states. So do the penalties—if you are caught driving over the limit—from extremely heavy fines to jail terms. A blood alcohol level over .05 percent could well lead to a fine and the loss of your driver's license. Most Australians who intend to drink will nominate a nondrinking driver, or else use taxis.

Taxis
As is the case anywhere in the world, taxis are not cheap. Fares vary from state to state. As the roughest guide to fares: in Sydney in 2003, flag-fall (turning on the meter) is $2.55, then you pay $1.45 per kilometer traveled, plus, if you made a telephone booking, a fee of $1.25. Taxi fares from the airports to the city centers are comparable. (There is, however, a train from inside Sydney airport to the Central Station.)

A lone passenger may choose to sit up front next to the driver. Most drivers are honest, though of course you should make sure that the meter goes on, and it is a good idea to note the driver's number, which is displayed above the windshield, in case you leave something behind when you alight. As a tip, give 10 or 15 percent, or round up the fare to the next dollar.

Taxi-driving is not a long-term profession, so you may well strike someone who is new to the job and not necessarily aware of the shortest route. It's worth checking a map yourself, for an idea of how to get to your destination. If you need to complain for any reason, you should call up the taxi company.

DRIVING IN THE OUTBACK

There are some important rules to note, particularly if you are planning to travel long distances from towns. If you break the rules, the consequences could be very serious. Plan your trip carefully, and get advice about every aspect.

Remember to take off the fan belt when driving through deep water to avoid splashing the engine's electrics. You will probably get through water in a creek or river provided that it does not come up much over the bottom of the car door. You must have someone—preferably someone who can swim—walking carefully ahead through creek beds and the like to indicate depths and muddy bottoms. (By the way, crocodiles do not much like running or flooding water.) If you do get stuck in mud or sand, first try letting the air pressure in your tires down so that they are nearly flat; put the car in second or third gear so as not to over rev; and drive using the hand-brake to stop the wheels from spinning. If this fails you will need to raise each rear wheel on the wheel-jack and place underneath them anything you can find to cover the mud or sand. Use cardboard boxes, branches, stones—anything on which your tires can get a grip.

DOS AND DON'TS

1. It is essential to have a reliable, good-sized, four-wheel-drive vehicle. Carry spare parts (and know how to fit them), spare gasoline, and water.
2. Have good road maps, and become familiar with them. Find out the state of the roads, particularly if you are going off well-used routes. Tracks through the outback can be very difficult. You should know the distance and timing of each day's journey, and the kind of weather (such as heavy rain or excessive heat) and anything else you are likely to experience.
3. Carry food and plenty of drinking water (this is most important).

If you are venturing into desert country, advise someone, preferably the police, of your destination and your estimated time of arrival. Arrange to call them to advise of your safe arrival.

If you break down, do not leave the car. Your chances of being seen or found are far better if you stay with your vehicle. Every year in the Australian outback someone leaves his or her car to walk for help and perishes, quite quickly, in the heat.

Hitchhiking

Hitchhiking is illegal in some states, but in any case it is best avoided, especially if you are alone, or even with a companion. Australia has had its share of hitchhiking rapes and murders.

ACCOMMODATION

Backpackers

In Australia the word "hostel" has mostly become "backpackers," or "backpacker hostel." Along with the name change has come a marked improvement in quality as well as quantity (they are to be found all over Australia). Many offer private rooms with *en-suite* bathrooms as well as small dormitories for groups of two to eight, and bigger ones for up to twenty. Some have bars and restaurants, twenty-four hour opening, tour booking facilities, laundry facilities, communal lounges, and general notice boards.

Backpacker hostels are cheaper than motels, guesthouses, "bed and breakfasts," and most hotels. They can stand alone, or be part of a pub or a caravan park. Wherever you are there will be Internet cafés to enable you to access e-mail accounts such as Hotmail or Yahoo. (You can set up a free account by going to www.hotmail.com or www.yahoo.com, and you will find a list of Australian Internet cafés.)

There are a number of backpacker hostel chains operating throughout Australia, including the YHA, YIP, NOMADS, YMCA, and YWCA.

Not So Cheap

If you want, and are prepared to pay for, something more than a backpacker hostel, there are various options. Throughout Australia there are hotels and motels with good, comfortable accommodation, with standards rising to luxury level. There are stringent government and local council controls, particularly in areas such as general cleanliness, and the storage, preparation, and supply of food.

All cities, larger towns, and tourist resorts offer first-class accommodation for businesspeople and other travelers. Of course, these are not generally cheap, but having said that, there are certainly some bargains to be had, and these are best sought out on the Internet.

There are "bed-and-breakfast" places throughout the country—but caution: these are not the equivalent of the modest "bed and breakfasts" found in Europe. Most of them offer accommodation of very high quality, complete with designer furnishings and expensive fittings. They are vastly superior to backpackers; in fact they are near the top of the accommodation hierarchy, and many of them also offer gourmet dinners at restaurant prices.

HEALTH AND SECURITY

The sun is often far more dangerous than the creatures mentioned below. You should *never* venture out in the sun without using a sun-block cream or lotion with a UV factor of 15 or higher (clearly marked on the package) applied to every exposed part of your skin—women should apply this routinely under their make-up. Also, you should never stay out in direct sun for more than a few minutes without a hat. Avoid the sun between 11:00 a.m. and 3:00 p.m. If you do get sunburned, you should immediately apply ice wrapped in a cloth (not directly), or get under cool running water. If it is serious, go to a doctor.

The availability of free health care varies

depending on your country of origin. As an intending visitor to Australia, especially if you are planning so stay for an extended time, you should check with your Embassy, and with an Australian Embassy or Consulate, to determine your travel insurance coverage. You should do this before you leave your country.

At the front of the telephone directory of each state capital (in the A-K volume for those states with two volumes), you'll find a great variety of health and other care organizations. Emergency services, public hospitals, narcotics anonymous, alcoholics anonymous, sexual assault counseling, suicide prevention, medical specialists, and community help for young people, are among the many services available to anyone in need.

Should you be in need of any help, do not hesitate to go to the nearest police station. You will find them very willing to assist you.

The Bush: Creepies and Crawlies
No kind of creature poses a greater or more constant threat to human well-being than we ourselves do. Compared to the harm that people do to each other, accidentally or maliciously, the impact of other species is seldom momentous. Yet it can be disquieting.

For animals to have power over us is an affront to our notions of environmental mastery, arousing emotions derived from a primitive fear—an inheritance from ancient man's struggle to survive in a world inhabited by many more dangerous creatures than exist today.

As a visitor to Australia you will be at far greater risk of being run over by a tour bus than of being bitten by anything very nasty. Many Australians have never seen a snake in its natural environment; few have encountered a funnel-web spider. With sensible care, you won't, either. These creatures live in their own environment, and it is only if you move into that environment that you will be at any risk at all, and then it will be minimal. Taking the following precautions will ensure your safety.

If you walk in the bush (the outback, rural land), keep to the well-traveled tracks, and you will almost certainly not meet any snakes. They much prefer their own company, and will keep away from the sound of walkers. They are sensitive to vibrations, will know you are coming a long time before you have any chance of seeing them, and will generally move out of the way. Very few attacks, according to the experts, are the result of treading on snakes in grass. Most result from acts of bravado or fear. People try to catch or harass them, when all they have to do is let them slip away. If you must move off well-traveled tracks, it is a good idea to carry a staff (a long stick) and occasionally hit the grass as you walk. But it is better not to tempt fate—have a happy holiday by being sensible and keeping to places where other people walk.

If you follow the above advice, you will not need to know the next bit—but it must be said. If the worst happens, and you are bitten, forget the old instructions about cutting the wound or sucking out the venom. Wrap a bandage firmly over the bite area and then up toward your heart, and get help or get to a doctor immediately.

If you are of a nervous disposition, don't read this paragraph. Many Australian snakes are venomous, and some are extremely potent. At least ten of them are more lethal than an Indian cobra. America's most feared rattlesnake would barely rank in Australia's top twenty.

There are lots of spiders; most of them are harmless, but some are poisonous. They are mostly in the bush, so if you are out walking or camping, be aware of them and where they are. Again, stay out of their area.

Be cautious of overhanging bushes or branches if you can't see clearly through them. Do not put your fingers under pieces of bark or wood, or turn stones over carelessly. Shift them slightly first, and then tilt them toward you so that you can see underneath, if you have to pick them up. As a general rule, don't touch spiders with bodies larger than your little fingernail. Better still, don't touch any of them. If one gets on your clothes, shake it off (don't brush it off with your hand). When picnicking or camping, shake out your blankets, groundsheets, sleeping bags, and the like. Check your shoes before you put them on. If one gets on your skin, take a deep breath and allow it to walk off—again, do not brush at it with your hand.

Once again, if you are nervous, don't read the following. The most dangerous (probably the world's deadliest) spider, the funnel-web spider, is found in the southern and eastern states. Most Australians have never seen one. These spiders like damp, dark undergrowth, away from tracks and paths, and venture out mostly at night. They can be deadly.

One spider that is found all around Australia (and is rarely deadly) is the redback—a small but nasty little creature that has taken to living in man-made structures and materials that people leave around—old tins, rubbish, fence-posts, and the like. Don't pick it up! There is antivenin available for both these and other spiders. If you should be bitten, bandage over the bite and toward your heart, and seek medical help *immediately.*

Walking

Similar rules apply elsewhere. On land, stick to
established paths and walkways. Wear solid
walking shoes or boots, and thick socks. Be
watchful in caves, and when walking under low
branches and through dense vegetation. Be careful
where you put your hands.

At the beach, it is generally safe to walk
barefoot on the sand, but before you do so look
and see whether other people are doing the same
thing. The swimming beaches you are likely to
visit will be quite safe, but make sure that you are
not venturing where the locals are not going.

It is not so safe to walk in water over rocks
without shoes and without care (never run—the
force of a running foot heightens the danger).
There are a couple of venomous creatures that
can inflict serious wounds. One, the stonefish, is
found mostly on coasts of Queensland, the
Northern Territory, and northern Western
Australia; the other, the blue-ringed octopus, may
be found in any rock pools on the coast. Go only
where you see the locals go.

The Sea—Here Be Monsters!

Not all these monsters are living. Rips (sudden
swirls of water racing out to sea), surf, and rocks
cause many more deaths than sharks. To avoid
these monsters, obey the following rules.

Never swim alone, and swim only on beaches manned by lifeguards, or where the local people are swimming with their children. Do not swim in surf if you are not used to it. You will probably see teenagers with surfboards, but you should note that they are accomplished surf swimmers, and often surf where it is not safe for visitors to swim. You should swim only in the area *between* the flags placed on the beach to show where it is safe, and patrolled, not outside the flags. Do not dive into the water from rocks, reefs, cliffs, or pontoons.

The Queensland and Northern Territory coasts are very dangerous from October to May. Check for jellyfish. A couple of these (the sea wasp and the box jellyfish) have virtually invisible tentacles that are capable of inflicting fatal stings.

Crocodiles are found year-round in northern Australia, inland in rivers and creeks, in estuaries, and on the coasts. They eat more than their fair share of tourists. Read up on any area you are visiting, and follow the advice of the locals. If there is no advice available, then don't swim.

Keep a sense of humor, follow the rules, and your holiday will be memorable for the right reasons. Happy traveling!

chapter eight

BUSINESS BRIEFING

"THE AUSTRALIAN WAY"

Business attitudes derive in part from the structures of the economy, their history, and the consequences of successive governments' attempts to control elements such as inflation, taxes, employment, and the like.

Before you venture into doing any business in Australia, it might be a good idea to familiarize yourself with some of the background, so that you will understand what has brought about "the Australian way." This will contribute to your business relationships and discussions with Australians, who have strong feelings for their links with the past, whether they and their families stem from early settlers or from more recent immigration.

The Australian economy has historically been seen to have a clear, cyclical, boom-bust pattern, in subdivisions such as the real estate market, the stock market, and interest rates. This might be lessening as successive Treasurers have searched for steadier development; however, the pattern is unlikely to disappear. To state the obvious but important fact, either you will arrive in a period of boom, with high real estate values and sales, strong stock market, relatively high interest rates, and so on, or you will hit a period of bust, with largely opposite indicators. It may be somewhere in between the two. You need to know! You should talk with the Trade Commissioner in your Australian Embassy or Consulate, or check on the Internet (see page 144).

A POCKET ECONOMIC HISTORY

The original settlers faced an unfamiliar, barren land, and struggled to produce enough food simply to feed themselves and their families. In the late eighteenth and early nineteenth centuries, large-scale sheep farming provided a new way of making a living. Land that would not support the

usual crops (mostly wheat, barley, and oats) was used as grazing land. It was said that the Australian economy "rode on the sheep's back." Wool was still the biggest export earner as recently as 1989.

   In the period from the 1820s, explorers and other pioneers found land suited to cattle raising, and many settlers started cattle stations (ranches).

The historical links with England provided a ready market for Australian wool, lamb, beef, and wheat.

For a long time Australia has been the Lucky Country. If you didn't grow it or graze it, you dug it up. Australia has vast mineral supplies and other natural resources: iron ore, gold, bauxite, oil, natural gas, zinc, lead, nickel, and copper—and

coal reserves for smelting. Of perhaps more interest than importance, Australia produces almost all of the world's opals, and large quantities of diamonds and sapphires.

More recently, Australia entered the technological world. In the late 1940s the Snowy Mountains Hydro-electric Scheme employed thousands of European immigrants in harnessing the waters of the Snowy River (on the border of New South Wales and Victoria) for the production of electricity and irrigation further downstream. In the same period, Australia built its first motor car, the Holden. Today, Holden cars are exported to the U.S.A., South Africa, and the Middle East. General MotorsHolden manufactures and exports car engines to various countries.

Australians are also resourceful on a small scale—they tend to invent things they can make in the back shed. Some of the more interesting of these inventions are described opposite.

Great Australian Firsts

The Stump Jump Plow

In 1870 a bolt broke from farmer Richard Smith's plow. He found that it then moved more easily over stumps and stones, so he went home and perfected the pivoting share that now slides over Australian farmland.

The "Ute"

In 1932, Lewis Brandt, a twenty-two-year-old Australian designer with the Ford Motor Company, drew up plans for a vehicle in which a farmer could take his family to church on Sunday and his pigs to market on Monday. It came to be called a utility truck, or "Ute," but back in Detroit Henry Ford called it a "kangaroo chaser."

Aspro

Pharmacist George Nicholas, in Melbourne, developed this pain reliever based on aspirin in 1917; by 1940 it had become the world's most widely used headache treatment.

Ultrasound

Developed in 1961 by scientists from the Commonwealth Health Department, this method of testing the health of unborn babies without X-rays is used around the world.

The Bionic Ear

In 1978 a team led by Professor Graeme Clark implanted a bundle of fine electrodes into the ear of a man who had become totally deaf in a car accident. After some months of fine tuning, he could hear again. A company called Cochlear Pty Ltd sells the technology to the world.

The Wine Cask

A plastic bag filled with wine inside a cardboard box was developed by Thomas Angove, the head of a South Australian wine company. These are now used worldwide.

The "Esky"

A company called Malleys saw the need in 1950 for a portable beer cooler. They made a steel box in a steel box that could be filled with iced water, and named it the "Eskimos." In the 1970s the esky became plastic—and could hold more beer.

Australia today is much less dependent on the export of primary products. In fact a very big market for the export of food to the U.K. was lost with their entry into the European Community. Other industries have taken its place. Tourism is a large and growing industry, and Australian universities cater to thousands of students from Southeast Asia. Service industries have grown to cope with local business requirements. The changes in economic emphasis, some recent and radical, to increased industrialization, have led to more openness in business attitudes. You will find Australian businessmen and women open to new ideas and recent developments. If you can show that you are informed about these developments, so much the better. As has been said, Australians work harder than business people in other developed countries, except for the U.S.A. and Japan. They are busy, and will not appreciate their time being wasted.

Organization charts tend to be flatter—less hierarchical—than is the case in some countries, such as France, Germany, and Japan. Senior decision makers are generally more accessible, particularly, but not only, in smaller companies. So, when seeking to present yourself, or your products, or services, go to the top. Find out who is the most senior person in your area and try to speak with him or her directly to make an appointment. If this is not possible, send an e-mail or brochure directly to that person.

WOMEN IN MANAGEMENT

Little needs to be said, apart from the fact that women are there. Women are in very senior management posts in Australia, and have long passed the need to prove their worth. It is very likely, if you become involved in business in Australia, that you will find yourself conducting your business with enterprising women.

THE WORK ETHIC

For some reason—perhaps partly because of their fondness for sport and for spending their weekends with their families—Australian workers have carried the stigma of being less than hardworking. It is also possible that this stemmed from the early power of the trade unions (see below), for over the last fifty years or more they strived for better work conditions, more appropriate working hours, and better pay rates, sometimes with militancy and calls for "All out!" ("drop tools, and leave the work area") that upset management, stockholders, and often the wives—the pay stopped!

Twenty or more years ago the phrase, "She'll be right" alluded not only to Australians' attitude to social life, but perhaps to work and business as well. Certainly union strikes and demarcation disputes (which worker from which union could do which job) were notorious, a way of life. And certainly workers won the right to advantages like the extraordinary "leave loading" (under which rules workers are paid more—a loading—when they are on holiday than when they are working). No more. Australians are "up there" with the U.S.A., Japan, and the U.K. in hours worked and, in a recent survey of sick days taken, "up there" in the lowest number of lost days. You can expect your business contacts to be hardworking—and they will expect you to be the same.

Australian workers, through their trade unions, won their basic rights over a long period of disputes and strikes. The eight-hour day was secured by striking stonemasons in 1855, the basic minimum wage in 1907, and the forty-hour week in 1946. The world's first legislation providing for paid sick leave and paid "long-service" leave was enacted in the state of New South Wales in 1951. You will find some Australians to be at once proud of the achievements of workers through their trade unions and, to a degree, disdainful of some of the union tactics. You will find a few workers who are very antimanagement, and some few managers who are scornful of the unions. But mostly you will find that workers are proud of their trades, and good at them, and that most managers respect the unions and are happy to be working with them.

While it is true that many Australians work to live (thinking that people from some countries seem to live to work), they work hard to achieve the life they have.

THE WORKING DAY

Normal office working hours are from 8:00 a.m. until 5:00 p.m. daily—no Saturdays. However, these vary; factors such as business requirements, customer needs, and traffic, are taken into account on a job-to-job basis. Banks are open slightly shorter hours—usually from 9:30 a.m. until 4:30 or 5:00 p.m. There is a move toward banks opening on Saturday mornings.

MAKING APPOINTMENTS

Personal relationships are important in doing business in Australia, especially for visiting businesspeople. The people you are wishing to meet will understand this, so if you have made a contact who could be helpful in getting you an appointment, ask him or her for help. However, you should be aware that although "helping" may extend this far, and may get you a friendly welcome, it does not extend to supporting your business or your proposition. Once in the interview, you are on your own.

Keep detailed notes on everyone you meet or hear referred to, and on their business and their roles. You may ask someone with whom you have gained an appointment if they can recommend someone else you should see, either in their own organization or in others.

Appointments should be made ahead by telephone. Ask for the person whom you wish to meet. You might be lucky, particularly in a smaller company, and be put straight through to speak to him or her, which would obviously be better than having to explain your position through a third party. However, it is quite likely that you will find yourself speaking to a personal assistant or secretary. Be ready to explain your position. Make it clear that you are a foreign visitor, and do not be afraid to ask for assistance. Most Australians will respond to a plea for help.

MEETINGS AND NEGOTIATION
There will be differences between big and small businesses, and these cannot really be established until you visit (unless you have information from

someone else). Many companies do business with overseas companies, and personnel in these companies are used to dealing with people from a range of cultures. They are likely to adapt quite readily to different kinds of humor, modes of address, and levels of formality.

It is standard business practice for men and women to wear a suit, but be prepared to take your jacket off if your host does so. Everyone shakes hands in business situations, and, unless dealing with very senior management or politicians, quickly moves to first-name terms.

Many people, particularly in creative circles, such as IT, publishing, advertising, and so on, now dress and operate in a much more informal way.

Offer your business card at the start of the meeting, and be prepared to answer questions such as, "How long have you been in Australia—and how do you like it so far?" However, casual and friendly as they might appear, Australian businessmen and women will want to get down to business, and will appreciate a readiness to do so. Outline your purpose in calling the meeting, and make your proposals with openness, directness, and brevity.

Australians accept negotiation as part of a business proposition. Be aware that, generally, you are negotiating from a position of weakness, in that you are on your host's home turf and playing by his or her rules. Listen and learn as quickly as possible just what the rules are—they will vary from company to company, and from individual to individual. Australians will be more impressed by your questions than by your statements. Be sure that you have gathered all available information before you begin to make your proposal. Be aware of your host's body language; if you do go too far in negotiation you will see a shift in attitude, such as tenseness in body, or terseness in language.

A sense of humor is invaluable. Many an exploratory question, suggestion, or offer can be made with humor and will be accepted in kind. Australians really appreciate people who can laugh at themselves, at their profession or occupation, or at their country. Be businesslike but relaxed.

MAKING A PRESENTATION

Keep your presentation factual, with details, specifications, and well-researched documentation. Australians often do not respond well to American-style "all singing all dancing" presentations—many of them work for American subsidiaries and suffer through them.

Big business houses and most of the smaller businesses will generally have up-to-date presentation equipment. If you are planning to show transparencies or need rear-view projection, for example, ask your contact at the company whether the necessary equipment could be made available for you to use. If there is any difficulty, then rent it.

Because you are a foreign visitor, and especially if what you are presenting is new to them, you can expect Australians to be concerned with historical data, testimonials, and references. Expect searching questions on business models used and data presented.

After or during your presentation you are likely to be questioned, and you will be expected to have done your homework in any areas that affect your proposal, such as customs, imports, money transfers, government regulations and approvals, and foreign investment; and also any relevant local issues, such as workplace agreements, industrial relations, and so on. It would be sensible to contact the Australian Trade Commission at the Australian Embassy or Consulate in your country before you leave home, to get the appropriate information and advice on such matters before preparing your presentation.

You might also find useful information on the Internet. The following Web sites might be helpful:

www.austrade.gov.au (Australian Trade Commission)

www.customs.gov.au (Import Trade Assistance)

www.dewr.com.au (Department of Employment and Workplace Relations)

www.oer.com.au (Australian Workplace Agreement)

EGALITARIANISM IN THE WORKPLACE

Australians do believe in equality—to a degree. This does not mean that they think workers on the factory floor should earn as much as senior managers, or that they should receive the same benefits. However, this is not because workers themselves, as individuals, are considered to be lesser beings, but just that the position they hold in the company does not make the same demands on them (in education, experience, qualification, and personal responsibility).

What are respected are individual ethics, work habits, general knowledge, and talents, along with success in relationships, effectiveness in child-raising—and the certain knowledge that senior managers in no way alone have these virtues. Thus, "Jack is as good as his master."

Friendships are often made across hierarchies—managers will play golf, sail, and have evening games of tennis with staff, even though such matters as income, politics, and lifestyle may separate them socially.

TRADE UNIONS

The Australian Council of Trade Unions (ACTU) supported Australian workers through the early years of disputes and strikes striving for basic rights regarding wages and conditions as early as 1855. The ACTU signed an Accord (the Prices and Income Accord) with the Australian Labor Party in 1983, when membership and activities were at a peak. From that time wages have been determined through a centralized and highly structured system of awards.

Since then, membership and aggressive union activities have declined. The average number of working days lost through disputes in the 1980s (about 1.5 million) was much less than in 1974 (6.3 million) Today, strikes are rare and generally short-lived. The influence of the ACTU (once an essential and powerful element in Labor politics) declined during the years of Labor government (through to the early 1990s) as right-wing dominance grew within that party.

With the Coalition (Liberal) government

having been in power for a number of years, and the Labor Opposition concerned that electors do not want a return to the days of industrial disputes, and therefore distancing themselves from the ACTU, today the power of the unions is declining.

However, the unions still have a role in business and management in Australia, in the protection of workers' rights. You would be well advised to find out what role that is in the companies you approach, and to understand the important part they have played in the Australian economy.

BUSINESS AND SOCIALIZING

Australians will tell you that the days of the "free lunch" are over. This alludes to the days when company entertainment of clients was tax-deductible as legitimate investment expenditure. These were known as the "palmy days," and many of the older managers remember them with nostalgia. Friday lunch was routine, and sometimes there was a lunch during the week. Afternoon drinks sealed many a deal, and golf was affordable. Not any more. You are over ten years too late.

Any drinking to which you are invited today will be private. Some company personnel, particularly in a small company, might invite you to lunch, or to a drink after work—but don't be disappointed if they don't. Such an invitation is the exception rather than the rule.

If you are invited to lunch, your hosts will be unlikely to drink alcohol, and you would be wise to follow suit. But if they do drink, and if your meeting has not been completed, a decision on your part to refuse alcohol will certainly be respected. On that note, if you don't drink alcohol, don't use this as a reason to refuse an invitation to a drink after work, or after the successful completion of an agreement. It will be accepted if you explain that you do not drink alcohol, and ask for something soft.

If you do find yourself at a club or pub with business associates, do not forget your "shout"— your turn to buy the drinks.

COMMUNICATING

AUSTRALIAN ENGLISH—SPEAKING "STRINE"

They speak English, don't they? Well, yes . . . but it is often a very special brand of English. The earliest Australian immigrants were a mixture of Irish and English convicts, soldiers (comprising a lot of Cockneys and other Londoners, a few north countrymen, and some Scots), and a number of educated naval officers. Then better-educated free settlers began to arrive, particularly in South Australia and Western Australia. This mixture of tongues has mutated into a general Australian English, or "Strine" ("Australian," said in Australian English), with some regional and elective differences. Rather than adding to or altering the language very much, later immigrants from Europe, and even later ones from Asia, have generally adopted Strine, but in keeping their own accents have often produced amazing results.

Be warned—it's very catching. Immigrants with children are often quite horrified, to begin with, when their children become fluent Strine speakers within months of meeting their new mates at school and playing with them "on Sat'di arvo" (on Saturday afternoon).

In an endeavor to capture the tone, actors from overseas are advised to raise the pitch a bit (speaking at a slightly higher level), breathe the words out through the nose, and end sentences with the upward lilt English normally reserves for questions. Try it, for fun—but caution: Strine is very individual, and is difficult to copy—it's better simply to let it happen. If you manage to master it you will be a hit at parties.

The accent is the butt of much humor, e.g.:
Patient to doctor: "Did I come here to die?"
Doctor: "No, mate, you came yesterdie."

The art of brevity, reducing any word to its diminutive, is an essential part of speaking Strine. Postman is usually "postie," car registration is "rego," journalist is "journo," musician is "muso." Even a U-turn (when driving a car) is a "u-ie." And we "chuck a u-ie" when we make a U-turn (chuck being to throw). "G'day mate," "ow yus goin?" and "Where's ya bin?" are diminutives of another type.

Names are also subject to diminution. Charles becomes Chuck, and when Prince Charles married Diana Spencer it was referred to as "the Chuck and Di show." Any man with red hair is, of course, called Blue, unless his name is Anthony, in which case he will be either Tone (diminutive overrides Blue) or Mark (Shakespeare shows sophistication and overrides most other things; and a man's wife who is seen as "a bit of a dragon" will be Lady Macbeth). Prince Philip is Phil the Greek. Anyone named Alexander is, of course, Brandy (from the drink Brandy Alexander), and all Warrens are called Rabbit.

You will find a glossary of Strine and some diminutives on pages 160–1.

TELEPHONE

> ### Emergencies
> Police, Ambulance, Fire—dial 000
> From a mobile—dial 112

Directories

The main communications carrier in Australia is Telstra. Each city has a Telstra White Pages telephone directory. In the larger cities, this runs to two volumes: A–K and L–Z.
Regardless of the number of volumes, the layout is roughly the same in all of them.

At the front of the directory (or at the front of the A–K volume) you will find:
Listings for federal, state, and local government services (traffic, health, education, aged care).
Emergency information.
Telephone information (phone cards, directory information, call costs, overseas calls).
Public transport information.

In the main section of each directory (spread across two volumes) you will find:
Business listings in alphabetical order.
Residential listings in alphabetical order.

At the back of each directory (or at the back of the L–Z volume) you will find:
Place-names and abbreviations.
International telephone codes.
Australian postcodes.

"Yellow Pages" is a directory of businesses, products, and services, containing emergency numbers, community services, essential services, help lines, rescue services, specialized health organizations, weather, boating, beaches.

Australia's telephone directories are also available on the Internet (www.whitepages.com.au and www.yellowpages.com.au).

Many businesses list their Internet addresses in the telephone directory. A number of specific Internet directories to be found online, and the company Citysearch (www.citysearch.com.au) produces an Internet directory both online and in book form.

Calling Home: Telstra
Australia uses the GSM mobile telephone system, and thus has compatibility with Europe and Asia, except for Japan, but not with the U.S.A.

Services
Information—White Pages telephone directory— business listings—Telstra.
Directory assistance national: 12455
Directory assistance international: 1225

Call Cards
For information, call toll-free1800 616 606. Prepaid calling cards, available from Telstra shops, newsdealers, and post offices, include "Say g'day" cards (cards and vouchers plus instruction booklet with access number for use on pay phones anywhere), and Telstra "Phone-away" cards, which have some advantages for particular calls. (Check with the retail outlet, or call the above number.) Internet: www.telstra.com.

FAX AND E-MAIL

Fax facilities, although fast becoming a thing of the past, are available in post offices, in most hotels, in many city and suburban printing and supply shops, and in public libraries.

E-mail and Internet services are available in Internet cafés in cities and suburbs.

POST

Australian post offices (with the insignia 'P' in a circle, white on red) are open between 9:00 a.m. and 5:00 p.m. throughout cities, suburbs, and country towns, in all states. Some open on Saturday mornings.

Next day postal services apply intrastate, and usually two-day services interstate (this may differ in country towns). There is usually one postal delivery per day in cities and metropolitan areas; the service is less frequent in some country towns and homes in the outback.

Poste restante mail (bearing the words "Poste Restante" followed by the address of a specified post office, which indicates that it should be kept there until collected—in the U.S.A. and Canada called "general delivery") can be collected from that post office during opening hours.

Post offices are retail outlets selling stamps, mailers (express and normal delivery), cards, toys,

and collector's items. Stamps are also available
from vending machines outside. Local residents
can pay some utility charges there. Banking is
available through Giro Post Banking—through
the Commonwealth Bank—you can find out
more from the outlets.

For information dial 13 13 17, or see White
Pages telephone directory—Australia Post.
Internet: www.auspost.com.au

COMMUNICATION STYLES

Australians generally (and it *is* a generalization)
dislike pretentiousness, and are unpretentious
themselves. Visitors do not have to prove
themselves. You are okay, mate!

As you have read, people from all over the
world have immigrated to Australia, have been
successful, have lived with jests at their expense
from "old" Australians, and have learned to join in
the humor.

Most Australians will prefer to get to know you
gradually. They would probably like to hear about
your background, education, areas of expertise,
special skills, and the like—but over a period of
time. They do not enjoy being confronted with
someone's achievements before having the
opportunity to accept and like them for who they
are. It is a lesson that some overseas folk, who

often seem to aggravate Australians, would do well to learn.

You don't have to prove anything—unless, of course, you forget your turn to shout, in which case you will quickly become a "bloody foreigner." On that note, it is worth remarking that some of what the rest of the world calls bad language or swearing has a different connotation and use in Australia. If you come from a polite background, and even if you come from certain countries, you may well be in for a shock.

The prime example is that great Australian adjective, "bloody." This causes great offense to some Americans, but it must be said that it does not carry any particular meaning in Australia. "Bloody" is simply a bit more colorful than its predecessor, "damned." What used to be "Close the damned door, will you?" has become, "Close the bloody door, will you?" It is simply an expletive, used for emphasis. It may suggest a lack of ability to use appropriate adjectives, but it is not meant to be offensive.

Even more paradoxical is the use (among males) of the word "bastard." You need to know that in Australia this is rarely an insult, being used warmly and humorously in such phrases as, "Bloody funny folk, these bastards!" "G'day, you old bastard!" and "How you goin', you old bastard?" These are, simply, affectionate greetings.

Women are rarely addressed in this way, and if they were it would almost certainly reflect on their birthright. Australian men readily use this kind of language with each other, but often have an old-fashioned dislike of using it to or in front of women. However, women also cheerfully swear.

The f∗∗∗ word (which is increasingly used by the younger generation) is still fundamentally taboo, as are some other unpleasant words.

Serious or Humorous?

Australians appreciate humor, both in business and socially. Given the choice, choose humor every time. Well, *nearly* every time. There is nothing funny about Australia losing a Test Match; don't laugh when a mate's wife runs away with the baker (it's not funny—unless of course she went with him for his "dough"), but you *may* congratulate him on his new-found freedom; and there is nothing funny about someone tipping over a perfectly good bottle of wine.

Really, there is very little that Australians do not make fun of. Their humor will often be sacrilegious; the freedom to satirize anyone is fundamental to democracy. Jokes made at the expense of certain minority groups, or those who are, or would be, unable to defend themselves, however, are considered offensive. Those in positions of power are fair game, and favorite targets are bishops, politicians, bosses, the police—and visitors. You should know that it is mandatory to be able to take a joke.

Few Australians would ever wear socks with sandals, and the European males who do so cause chuckles. On a more serious note, Australians have largely overcome their early difficulty in accepting taxi drivers in turbans. Even more seriously, some Australians object to women wearing a veil or scarf. This is from ignorance; it is not general, and will change with time and education. If you wear such apparel, be aware that most Australians will accept your right to do so.

There is a time in business dealings to forgo the humor. For you, that is. Your host will retain the right to have a joke at your expense, in which case you can join in with a quick retort—but only if you can think of a good one.

Most Australians reckon that it's a poor day if you can't have a laugh.

CONCLUSION

So you are going to Australia, and, yes, it is a long way to go. But your visit can offer such rich rewards that it shouldn't be missed. As you have seen, a traveler will find very little sameness. Diversity is the hallmark of Australia and of Australian life.

Australia is still a member of the British Commonwealth. About 50 percent of Australians are monarchists, and emotional links with the "mother country" are strong. However, immigration has brought with it emotional ties to many other European and Asian countries.

Not so fixed are the economic links. Since the formation of the European Economic Community, Australia has lost much of its European export market and has turned to Southeast Asia. Japan is now the biggest foreign investor in Australia, mainly through massive tourism and property investment, much of it in Queensland. In the 1980s, Asia took about half of Australia's exports. These have lessened recently, while exports to the U.S.A. have grown hugely. The key to Australia's psyche is, again, diversity—of cultural, emotional, and economic links.

In this book you have read of certain Australian characteristics. The Australians do work to live—but remember, if you should join the workforce, they work hard at their jobs too. They allow full rein to their sense of humor, and it will often be at your expense—but generally only if they like you. They tend to be egalitarian—as a visitor to their home you will be made extremely welcome—as long as you do not tell them for a while that you are very wealthy, very educated, very talented, or very important.

But, beyond all that, Australians are very *human,* in the sense that, like all of us, they are proud of their country. They want you to enjoy it, and they like hearing appreciation expressed by visitors. If you like something, tell them.

Australians tend also to be honest and unpretentious. After you get to know them it will be understood that you may find some things difficult to enjoy. Use some humor, and you will be able to express this too.

Because Australia and Australians are generally welcoming and visitor-friendly, wherever you go, you should try to see and enjoy as much as you can in whatever time you have. Even before you start out, well before you arrive, you are a welcome visitor.

"Enjoy" is the key word. Keep a sense of humor, be eager and interested in your exploration, and you will be met with humor and an interest in *you.* Making friends is inevitable.

Glossary: Strine, and Some Diminutives

Akubra
Classic, broad-brimmed Aussie hat

Arvo
Afternoon, as in "see you Sat'di arvo"

Barbie, bar-b-que
Barbecue. Out-of-doors cooking, mostly meat

Bathers
also swimmers, togs, cossie. Swimming costume

Battler
Worker. Aussie concept of struggler, underdog

Beaut
Great, wonderful

Bludger
Usually "dole-bludger," one living off unemployment benefits

Bottle shop
Wine/beer shop, liquor store

Brickie
Bricklayer

Chook
Chicken, as in "chook raffle" (raffling a chicken)

Chrissie
Christmas

Cobber
Old word for a mate, little used today

Cocky
Farmer or shepherd

Compo
Compensation, as in worker's compensation

Crook
Ill, sick

Crust
Livelihood, as in bread and butter: "making a crust"

Deli
Delicatessen

Dinkum
Honest, true, as in "fair dinkum"

Dob in
Inform on someone, betray

Dough
Money (bread is also money)

Dunny
Outdoors toilet, WC

Esky
Portable cooler for food and drink

Footie
Football—the ball and the game

Globe
Light bulb

Gong
Medal

Grog
Liquor, booze

Jackaroo, Jackeroo
(female, Jillaroo). Working rider on a farm

Jarmies
Pajamas

Layby
Purchase by installments;
the goods stay in store
until paid for

Larrikin
(usually kindly). Scallywag,
mischievous

Ocker
The ultimate uncultured
Australian, with beer belly
and thongs (sandals)

Pokey
Poker machine, slot
machine

Poofter
Derogatory term for male
homosexual

Prezzie
A present

Ratbag
Stupid person

Root
Be careful. Fairly and little-
used word for sexual
intercourse

Sandgroper
Western Australian,
because of the deserts

Sheila
Girl (old slang term)

Shout
Buy a round of drinks

Sickie
A day taken off from work
because of sickness

Smoko
Smoke, as in taking a
smoking break at work

Spit the dummy
Lose your temper

Strides
Trousers

Stubby
Small bottle of beer, or
men's shorts

Swag
Bag or bundle carried by a
"swagman," or bush
traveler, as in the song
"Waltzing Matilda"

Tassie
Tasmania

Throw a wobbly
Lose control of yourself

Tinnie, Tube
Can of beer

Uni
University

Whinger
Complainer, especially as
in "Pommy whinger"

Wowser
Puritan, killjoy

culture smart! australia

Resources
Emergency (police, fire, ambulance) 000; from a mobile 112

Health and Safety
Poisons Information Centre 13 1126
Police for nonemergency situtations 13 1444
St. John Ambulance Australia (Flying Doctor service, first-aid courses, and
information) (02) 9241 2411; www.stjohn.org.au

At the front of the telephone directory in each state (A-L where applicable)
are lists of health and other care organizations. These include Public
Hospitals, Narcotics Anonymous, Alcoholics Anonymous, Sexual
Assault Counseling, Suicide Prevention, Medical Specialists, and
Community Help for Young People.

TIS Translating and Interpreting Service 13 1450

Air Travel
Qantas 13 1313; www.qantas.com.au
Virgin 13 6789; www.virginblue.com.au
Flight Centre (02) 9286 3638. This is an Australia-wide travel operator with
a subsidiary company, Student Flights, that has cheap air fares for
students and backpackers. Shop 32, Town Hall Arcade, 464-480, Sydney
2000 (arcade next to Town Hall railway station).

Coach Travel
Greyhound Pioneer 13 2030; www.greyhound.com.au
McCafferty's 13 1499; www.mccaffertys.com.au

Ferry Travel
Boat Torque Cruises (Rottnest Island) (08)9430 5844;
www.boattorque.com.au

Rail Travel
Rail Australia (08) 8213 4592; www.railaustralia.com.au

Car Rental
Avis 13 63333; www.avis.com
Budget 1300 362 848; www.budget.com.au
Europcar 13 1390; www.deltaeuropcar.com.au
Hertz 13 3039; www.hertz.com
Thrifty 1300 367 227; www.thrifty.com.au

Roadside assist/motoring organizations
Australian Capital Territory and New South Wales(NRMA) 13 2132;
www.nrma.com.au
Northern Territory (AANT) (08) 8981 3837; www.aant.com.au
Queensland (RQCQ) 13 1950; www.racq.com.au
South Australia (RAA) (08) 8202 4600; www.raa.net
Tasmania (RACT) (03) 6232 6300; www.ract.com.au

Western Australia (RAC) 13 1704; www.rac.com.au
Victoria (RACV) 13 1955; www.racv.com.au

Accommodation
Allbackpackers, Nick Downing, P.O. Box 494, Elsternwick, Victoria, 3185
www.allbackpackers.com.au

On the Internet, try Google or Alta Vista for "Australia hotels" or
    "Backpackers Australia" —travelers' information—or—Wizard of Oz
    backpackers (based in Coogee, Sydney, they list locations, rooms,
    facilities, services, nightlife, prices, bookings, and available work).
    "YHA Australia" suggests backpacker and youth hostel accommodation
    and travel and offers maps, travel deals, and advice.

Travelers with Disabilities
National Information Communications Awareness Network 1800 806 769;
    www.nican.com.au

Lost or Stolen Credit Cards
Banks
ANZ 1800 033 844
Citybank 13 2484
Commonwealth 13 2221
National 1800 033 103
St George 1800 028 208
Westpac 1300 651 089
Card organizations
Visa (local cardholders) 1800 450 346
Visa (international cardholders) 1800 805 346
American Express 1300 132 639

Further Useful Web Sites
Australian Broadcasting Corporation: www.abc.net.au
Australian Job Search: www.jobsearch.com.au
Australian Trade Commission: www.austrade.gov.au
Australian Workplace Agreement: www.oer.com.au
Australia's Internet and Phone Directory: www.citysearch.com.au
Department of Employment and Workplace Relations: www.dewr.com.au
Department of Immigration: www.immi.gov.au
Import Trade Assistance: www.customs.gov.au
Overseas Trade Skills Assessment: www.workplace.gov.au
Reciprocal health insurance cover: www.hic.gov.au—Travelers to
    Australia—rhca
Special Broadcasting Services: www.sbs.com.au.
Telstra: www.telstra.com
White pages: www.whitepages.com.au
Yellow pages: www.yellowpages.com.au

There are plenty of Internet cafés in Australia. You can set up a free account
by going to www.hotmail.com or www.yahoo.com.

Further Reading

History and Contemporary Affairs
Blainey, Geoffrey. *The Tyranny of Distance*.
Australia: Sun Books, 1975.
Australia's history shaped by its geography and size.

Blainey, Geoffrey. *A Shorter History of Australia*.
Melbourne: Heinemann, 1994.

Chatwin, Bruce. *The Songlines*.
London: Jonathan Cape, 1988.
Insight into Aboriginal beliefs.

Clark, Manning. *A Short History of Australia*.
New York: Penguin, 1981.
The picture up to the 1980s (the full version is in six volumes).

Daly, Margo, et al. *The Rough Guide to Australia*.
London: Rough Guides, 2001.

Harding, Paul, et al. *Lonely Planet: Australia*.
Melbourne/Oakland/London/Paris: Lonely Planet Publications, 2002.

Horne, Donald. *The Lucky Country: Australia in the Sixties*.
Ringwood, Victoria, Australia: Penguin, 1964.
The definitive study reference to Australia.

Morgan, Sally. *My Place*.
New York: Henry Holt, 1988.
London: Virago, 1988.
Biography.

Pilger, John. *A Secret Country*.
London: Jonathan Cape, 1992.
Pilger is Australia's (and other parts of the world's) conscience. He shows the other side of contemporary Australia.

Pusey, Michael. *The Experience of Middle Australia*.
Cambridge: Cambridge University Press, 2003.
The effects of economic globalization and economic rationalism on middle Australia.

Reynolds, Henry. *The Other Side of the Frontier.*
Townsville: James Cook University, 1981.
Ringwood, Victoria, Australia: Penguin, 1982.
White settlement of Australia—the Aborigine's view.

Sharp, Ilsa. *Culture Shock! Australia: A Guide to Customs and Etiquette.*
Portland, Oregon: Graphic Arts Center Publishing, 2000/London:
Kuperard, 2002.

Summers, Ann. *Damned Whores and God's Police.*
Ringwood, Victoria, Australia: Penguin, 2001.
Describes the attitude of the authorities to female convicts and free
settlers and explores the influence of this on the colonies and on
modern Australia.

Fiction
David Malouf. *Johnno*, and other works
Frank Hardy. *Power Without Glory*
Richard Flanagan. *Sound of One Hand Clapping*
Elizabeth Jolley. *My Father's Moon*
Tim Winton. *Cloudstreet*

culture smart! australia

Index

culture smart! australia

Acknowledgment

I would like to thank Beth Kennedy for her untiring and incisive critiques of the manuscript for this book, and her valuable advice for its improvement.